Telling Stories, Te

Telling **Stories,** Telling **Lives**

ANN LLOYD

DARTON · LONGMAN + TODD

First published in 2005 by
Darton, Longman and Todd Ltd
1 Spencer Court
140–142 Wandsworth High Street
London SW18 4JJ

ISBN 0 232 52525 0

A catalogue record for this book is available from the British Library.

Designed and produced by Sandie Boccacci
using QuarkXPress on an Apple G5 PowerMac
Set in 11/14pt Apollo
Printed and bound in Great Britain by
Page Bros, Norwich, Norfolk

This book is dedicated, with many many thanks and much affection, to my five interviewees:

Wesley Carr, Gerard Hughes, Linda Mary, Philip Newell and Linda Riley.

Contents

If we are not in touch with our own stories,
we can't be in touch with God.

Gerard W. Hughes

Introduction

Most days I practise writing as a musician practises scales. I took up the suggestion of Julia Cameron, in her book *The Vein of Gold,* to write morning pages. I write longhand until I've filled three pages of foolscap paper. It usually takes somewhere between 20 and 30 minutes.

Once a notebook is filled I throw it away and start on the next one. Usually the pages are full of shopping lists, rants in which I finish rows with me winning instead of losing because I just don't think fast enough, and as much as I can remember of my dreams.

But whenever there is something on my mind, it inevitably finds itself on paper before I have reached the bottom of the third page. It's a good emotional clear-out exercise. And very very occasionally I find myself writing something interesting. As on the day I was thinking about a conference at Farnham in 1982, which led me to think of reading *God of Surprises,* which in turn led me to ponder on the significance of a retreat I'd attended in 1998. Then, before I even knew I had been thinking it, there on the page was the idea for this book: wouldn't it be great to interview the people who had influenced the direction of my inner journey about the people, places and events that had influenced them, and weave their stories in with mine? I really liked the idea of a whole network of interconnecting threads stretching between lots and lots of people.

I took the idea to Darton, Longman and Todd and here,

five years later, is the book which started its life as a scribble in my morning pages.

I recommend the exercise of thinking back to the people who've been your influences to everyone. Apart from anything else, it makes you aware of the people you really need to thank. I take the opportunity now to thank my five interviewees, for the deeply significant part they have all played in helping me find my way.

I want also to say a special thank you to Brendan Walsh, Editorial Director at Darton, Longman and Todd, for his continuing commitment to the book and his unwavering support and encouragement.

Chapter 1

Sin, originally

My very first teacher at St Benedict's is Miss Mortimer. She's not a frightening teacher like Mr Moore: she's nice, she never gives anybody the strap. She has thick, bushy golden-red hair and a jolly, plump face. Her skin is white like flour except for her red cheeks. Today she is wearing her bottle-green cardigan with a white blouse and a dark green tartan skirt with bits of yellow in it. The first class every day is religious and today Miss Mortimer is beginning by pinning a big white piece of paper to the blackboard. She's never done that before. We all watch, wondering what she's going to do next.

Now she is drawing with a thick black crayon on the shiny white paper. A big black circle. She turns to look at us, her eyes moving from one end of the classroom to the other. In the sunlight that slants through the windows I can see hundreds and thousands of tiny specks floating in the air. She points at the circle.

'This is the soul.'

We look from her to the black outline of the circle and then back to her. She looks at us some more. Then she turns her back and does something to the circle. When she stands to one side we can see that now there are little pin-points of black inside the white circle. Like when the rain makes tiny holes in crusty snow.

'Every one of you,' says Miss Mortimer, looking at each of us in turn, 'everybody, has a soul. But you can't see it because it's so deep in the middle of you, right in the very middle.'

She pulls back her chin so that her neck makes another chin underneath it.

'Now then, who can tell me what the little black dots are?' Silence.

'Well,' she points at all the little black dots again, 'these are all venial sins. Venial,' she repeats, saying the first bit of the word, 'VEN-ial', very loud. Nobody speaks, nobody even wriggles.

'And, when you are disobedient, or late for Mass, or don't say your morning or evening prayers, this is what happens. These little black dots appear on your soul. They are called venial because they are little.'

She turns back to the board again. Now some of the little black dots are the size of Smarties.

'Yes,' nods Miss Mortimer, 'these are bigger sins.'

She studies them gravely, as we do. Have I got any big black dots on my soul? How do you know? Can the little ones all lump together to make a big one? I try to remember if I've *ever* said my morning and evening prayers. And how many times, since he started taking me to Mass, have me and my Dad been late?

But Miss Mortimer is speaking again.

'Now we don't want any of these on our souls, do we?' She shakes her head slowly and deliberately from side to side.

'No, we don't, do we?'

We in our turn shake our heads, equally slowly and deliberately. There are lots of 'No, Miss's whispered from around the class.

She moves towards the board again. The circle is now completely black. You could have heard a hankie drop onto the wooden floorboards.

'And this is what happens if you commit a MORTAL sin. If you commit a mortal sin, which is the biggest sin of all, your whole soul is black. And when it is all black it is gone. All gone. It is dead. It is dead because of your mortal sin. You have lost your soul.'

She pauses to look at us all, sitting like little statues in the silence. Only her eyes and the dust specks are moving through the shafts of sunlight that slant through the window.

'Now, who can tell me what happens if your soul is all black like this when you die?'

'Please, Miss.'

Marian Fairhurst has her hand up.

'Yes, Marian?'

'Please, Miss, you go to hell for ever and ever and ever and ever.'

'Yes, Marian, that's right. You go to hell for ever.'

Marian looks round in triumph.

'I know because I heard my Dad tell my Mum that if—'

'That's enough, Marian!'

'Yes, Miss.'

'So, what must we all—'

The bell rings for the end of class, interrupting Miss Mortimer and making me jump.

She waits for it to finish, her glance keeping us at our desks.

'We must keep our souls clean, mustn't we?'

'Yes, Miss.'

She looks at us all again, very serious.

'All right, off you go.'

A mad scramble for the door.

'And no running,' she shouts, and then lowers her voice to tell us to walk.

Chapter 2

A surprise at the National Museum

August 1967. Athens. My first trip to Greece. I should have been in heaven. I wasn't. I was bored and bad-tempered. Athens in August, I had discovered, was suffocatingly hot, sticky, dusty, and very noisy.

It all started with the film, *Zorba the Greek*. I had loved it, and had even stayed to watch all the credits roll past, instead of dashing out to the pub as soon as 'The End' appeared on the screen. I noticed that it was based on a book by someone I'd never heard of, with an unpronounceable name: Kazantsakis. I bought the book. I was even more enraptured than I had been with the film. Alexis Zorba – and by extension the Greeks – seemed to me to have just about got it right: he lived every day as if he would die the next, asked his boss questions like, 'If your books don't tell you why men have to die, what use are they?' and ended up teaching this same boss how to dance. By the sea. And the dancing ... and the music. Wow. There was no doubt about it: I had to go to Greece.

At first I planned to hitchhike. I'd hitched on my own from home, Hindley, in Lancashire, to Paris a couple of years earlier and loved it, so was really looking forward to the trip through France, Italy, and Yugoslavia to Athens. The destination had to be Athens because it was the only place I'd ever heard of in Greece. A couple of weeks before I was due to leave, however, my boyfriend, who lived in Surrey, wrote to say he had decided to go to Athens. He'd take his car, I could go with him. The car, a mini, had broken down in Nis, in back-of-beyond Yugoslavia and was now on its way back to England. So I got my first sight of the Parthenon from the third class carriage of a Yugoslavian train. It looked so precisely, so exactly, as I had pictured it that I couldn't believe it was real.

The evenings were OK: we went to the plaka, ate and drank and watched the Greeks dance and smash plates. But once we'd been to the Parthenon a couple of times the days began to drag; we didn't know what to do with ourselves. On this particular afternoon, which was even more humid than usual, we'd wandered further from the centre of town and come across the National Museum. Although neither of us were enthusiastic about museums, we decided it would at least be cooler inside. And it was free.

Once inside the museum we soon went off in different directions, and after about ten or fifteen minutes of drifting around in the quiet of the tall-ceilinged marble rooms I found myself in front of a row of terracotta statues. They all looked the same. They all had the same angular flat planes for bodies and smoothly rounded heads. They all looked young and sweet. They all had the same charming smiles. I smiled back at them, as I leaned forward to read the information card. This told me that their arms were attached to their sides at the wrists because at the time they were made the sculptors didn't know how to make arms that were free of the body: they had been afraid that if the arms weren't attached to the body at the wrists they would drop off. I glanced back at the statues: each one had a small block or bridge pinning its wrist to its thigh. So there they all stood, neatly in their row, smiling sightlessly, but sweetly, their arms at their sides.

There were no doors in the museum so as I turned to go into the next room I saw straight away what it contained. I stopped dead where I stood. For several seconds I just stood and stared, as incapable of movement as the row of statues behind me. Then I felt hot tears fill my eyes and begin to spill down my cheeks. I took a deep, deep breath.

What I was looking at was a towering bronze statue of Poseidon, the god of the sea. It was impressive enough in its beauty and sheer size, especially coming after the neat row of motionless terracotta statues. But what had first of all transfixed me and then brought me to tears were Poseidon's arms: they were stretched straight out from the shoulders. Horizontal. Straight out into the air.

The tears continued to pour down my face but now I was smiling as well, grinning, my heart thumping in my chest.

When I was finally able to pull my gaze from the statue I noticed that the room was almost empty, which was perhaps as well because had it been full, somebody might have wondered if I was in need of medical attention, standing there staring, my jaw dropped, crying and almost laughing at the same time.

I felt I would burst if I didn't share this with somebody. With a last, smiling, grateful glance at Poseidon, I dashed off to look for my boyfriend. I found him sitting in the shade in the museum's garden, with a jug of lemonade. I babbled it all out: the arms, pinned, not now, Greeks, free, arms free, out, out in the air. Tears pricked at my eyes again and my throat tightened as I told him. He listened, nodded and shrugged. I sat back, frowning at him. He didn't understand. I hadn't made him understand. He opened his newspaper and began to read. But was it so surprising that he didn't understand, when I didn't understand myself? I didn't understand and I'd been there. I couldn't stop returning to the experience, turning it over and over, examining it from every angle. Finally, exhausted by my fascination, I had to give up. I had to give up and just accept that this mysterious event was, well, a mystery.

Chapter 3

Why pray?

This was what was written on the whiteboard which confronted us as we took our places in a large sun-filled room
at Farnham Castle in Surrey, in May 1982, for the first day
of a week-long conference on the spiritual aspects of the
work of an Anglican charity, The Missions to Seamen.
Mission chaplains, who are based in ports around the
world, looking after the needs of seafarers, got together for
such a meeting every two years. I was there because I was
working in the charity's PR department.

The conference was to be led by Dr Wesley Carr, the
Canon Residentiary of Chelmsford and Director of Training
in the diocese, now Dean of Westminster Abbey, and his
colleague Canon Peter Marshall, now Dean of Worcester. I'd
only just started work at the Mission, in 1980, when I'd first
heard his name; that had been after everyone came back
from the previous conference, which he had also led. I had
been curious about him ever since.

The curiosity arose as a result of the way people who had
attended that 1980 conference had reacted to him. There'd
been agitation, excitement, and strong emotions. Was there
anger among those emotions? It felt as if you might be on
dangerous ground if you probed too much. I was intrigued
to know why, and how, he had provoked such a turbulent
and powerful response; but no one seemed able to put it
into words.

Why pray?

It was only when I met Wesley Carr, the evening before the conference began, that I realised I had formed an image of him in my head over the preceding two years. The person I met was around forty, I guessed, serious, self-contained and thoughtful. The image that had formed in my head however, was rather different. That was of a seventy-something, fire and brimstone Old Testament prophet type of preacher, with flowing white hair and beard to match: a real thunderer. Such a priest would have frightened me; did the image mean I had inferred fear in the response to Wesley Carr? I just didn't know; didn't quite know what to think.

At that first 'Why pray?' session he talked to us about prayer, and said that afterwards we would split into groups to discuss our answer to the question 'Why pray?', and would each write our (anonymous) responses on posters, which would be pinned up at the front of the room so that we could all discuss them. I can't remember all that he said but I can remember feeling enlivened by it. One thing I do remember is that he made it clear he did not want 'baby answers' such as 'because Christ told us to'. He wanted us to address the question very seriously, to think deeply and honestly about it. He also asked us to reflect on whether, when we prayed, we considered ourselves to be alone, or not.

At the end of the talk I bounced up from my seat and turned to my old friend, who was also my boss in the PR department, and offered 'Well, why not pray?' as a possible answer, thinking myself rather clever. In spite of this would-be smart and superficial response, however, I was actually very excited that someone had given voice to this question and that I now had the chance to discuss it with other people. I found prayer extremely difficult: had done for years, ever since leaving childhood behind, in fact. I wasn't sure what I was doing when I did it, nor did I know if I really meant it anyway. I had decided some years earlier

9

that praying for anything except strength was probably a waste of time, and that 'asking for things' was childish and surely not what prayer was about.

As for being alone or not when you prayed, well, that was some question: was God personal or not? And if not, what? Why pray?: a single question that took you straight to the questions at the heart of faith: who or what was God and what was your relationship to him/it?

To tell the truth, I hadn't done much praying for some years. I'd converted to Anglicanism in 1972 to get away from being labelled a lapsed Catholic, which enraged me because of its implicit assumption that you could only either be a Roman Catholic or a lapsed Roman Catholic: that is, that you could not choose to stop being a Roman Catholic.

I had hoped to find a spiritual home in the Anglican Church, but over the ten years since 1972 I had gone to Communion less and less, been put off by sermons more and more, and been bored by the formality of the services. Going to church had begun to feel very thin and mechanical, somehow. Something was not right. Also I felt I had nothing in common with people I saw at services. I watched them kneeling down, standing up, sitting, going to Communion. And I knelt and stood and sat and went to Communion with them, all the while observing myself doing all this, and praying that taking part with only half a mind and heart wouldn't be disrespectful to God. Most of the time I didn't feel anything apart from dry and tired; I'd given up on any sort of searching for God. Not knowing where else to look or what else to do I had, I suppose, unconsciously switched off at some deep level. But this question, 'Why pray?' had stirred something at that deep level, which, if I'd thought about it at all, I had assumed was dead.

The group seemed less affected by the question than I was and with the exception of one chaplain seemed not to have any problems with prayer. We did decide that we couldn't put our response into words and settled on drawing two pairs of hands on our poster: God's in the top left corner, if I remember rightly, and ours towards the lower right. I did manage to persuade the others, however, that there should be a very big gap between these sets of hands, to show the distance, the great gulf that had somehow to be crossed in any attempt at communication between them. I wanted the strain to show but just couldn't think how to do it, and anyway, I reasoned, if the group as a whole wasn't finding prayer a real strain then the poster should show that, not the position of one member of the group. We settled on the big distance between the hands.

Dr Carr was scathing about our sentimental and superficial attempts to answer, or perhaps avoid answering, the question. He was particularly dismissive of my group's offering (though, of course, none of the posters were identified by group) with its anthropomorphic sets of hands reaching for hands. I opened my mouth to protest that we had meant to show distance and strain and had avoided words because of their inadequacy but by the time I had made my half-hearted attempt to catch his eye (after all, I was the only one in my group who had wanted to suggest there was a real sense of strain) the discussion, which had become somewhat heated, had moved on.

There was a sense of confrontation between the group and Dr Carr and his assistant now. I was thoughtful and serious, knowing something important was happening but not knowing what it was. The questions, 'Why pray?' and whether you were alone or not when you did were still very much around.

The next day Dr Carr began by reminding the conference

that he and his colleague were acting with integrity. This struck me as very odd because it seemed something beyond dispute. The air of confrontation was still there. That evening, the reading during the short evening service in the chapel was given by a bishop who was attending the conference with us. It was all about peace and harmony. It bothered me more than the feelings of confrontation during the day.

At the session the following morning Dr Carr asked for comments on the course of the conference so far, and I suddenly saw what it was that had bothered me about the prayer the bishop had said the previous evening: it ran counter to the direction of the conference. I stuck up my hand and made my comment. That I did so without any nervousness should have amazed me as I hate speaking up in a crowd, but it didn't. My remark led to a suggestion from someone on the other side of the room, whom I couldn't see, that perhaps I would like to choose a suitable passage and read it at that evening's service.

The suggestion felt like a challenge: combative, maybe even punitive. I agreed. Again, normally I would have avoided doing any such thing, fearing to make a fool of myself by making some sort of mistake in public. Another reason for panic would have been because I wouldn't have had much of a clue as to where to find an appropriate reading. I quickly realised, however, that I had just the reading I needed. And as the day went on the perception that something had changed radically for me formed and deepened. It sprang from the lack of timidity both in making my initial comment and then my lack of apprehension about the coming reading in chapel. Perhaps most people would not be so nervous. Nevertheless, I was normally apprehensive and uncomfortable about such things. But not now. I wasn't being brave when I spoke out; I was not having to damp down feelings of panic about getting up and reading in chapel. I was just simply completely OK with it. Where this energy and confidence had come from I didn't know, but I couldn't doubt it. And I knew that although I didn't understand it it had everything to do with difficult and big questions being directly asked. There was a feeling of coming back to life: as if an 'engine' that had been dead was being kick-started back into life. All of a sudden I was up and running again and it felt wonderful.

What I read was taken from *The Plain Man Looks at the Beatitudes* by William Barclay, which I had brought with me to the conference. I had just read chapter 9, 'The bliss of the breaker down of barriers', on the beatitude 'Blessed are the peacemakers, for they shall be called the children of God' (Matthew 5:9).

> We must mark one all-important fact in this Beatitude – the people to whom the blessing is promised. The people who are blessed are not the peace-*lovers* but the peace-*makers*. It can happen that a man is a peaceful man and a peace-lover, and is yet not a peacemaker. A man may know that there is something wrong in some situation, in his family, in his church, in some group of which he is a member; he may know that something ought to be done to rectify the situation; but he may also know that any step taken to mend the situation may well involve difficulty and trouble and problems which it will not be pleasant to face. In such a situation a man may well decide to do and say nothing, as he will put it, 'for peace's sake '... He will allow the situation to continue and the whole matter to drift uneasily on, because his love of a certain kind of peace makes him evade all trouble. Such a man may be called a peaceable man and a peace-lover;

but he is certainly not a peace-maker; he is rather in the end a trouble-maker; for the longer any situation is allowed to continue the more serious its consequences and the harder its cure. The man who is blessed is the man who is prepared to face difficulty, unpleasantness, unpopularity, trouble in order to *make* peace.[1]

Dr Carr and I met again twenty-one years later, in 2003, in the Dean's study at Westminster Abbey: a wonderfully quiet and still place, it seemed to me. I found it difficult to believe that we were sitting talking only yards from the crowds of tourists getting down from their buses, adding more noise and confusion to the din and rush of central London.

'The first thing I can remember was the war: by the end of it I was old enough to watch the bombs falling over London ... But I suppose the two most important facts at the beginning of my life were that first of all I was born to parents who were Salvation Army officers, who remained so right to the end of their lives, and second that we moved when I was small to Beckenham, Kent (now South London), where there was no Salvation Army. Because of that I went to the local church, attended Sunday School, joined the cubs and then the choir, and ended up pretty well embedded in the Church of England.

'One of the questions I often ask myself is if there hadn't been that experience of church, Sunday School, cubs, choir, and the woman next door hadn't been a Church of England Sunday School teacher but, say, a Baptist, for

---

[1] William Barclay, *A Plain Man Looks at the Beatitudes* (Fount, 1985).

instance, what would I have been? I might have become a Baptist, I don't know.'

The way he says this, reflectively and with a half smile, lets you know that he doesn't ask himself this question with any kind of agony or urgency, but rather with a simple curiosity about how his path might have been different.

'I do tend to think,' he continues after a moment's silence, 'that I am Anglican naturally, by nature, by temperament: I slid into the ethos very easily without even thinking about it, it just seemed completely natural.'

His parents didn't mind much at all, he says. 'I think in the end my father was sort of more Anglican than my mother, who was very Salvationist. I don't think my mother ever understood what I was really about being a priest, Church of England and so on: she just thought I was doing good. I hope.'

He was lucky in that he 'just hit that point in history when education was being offered on scholarships. I had a great chance in my life at that point which I think other people have been denied since'. He got a scholarship to Dulwich College where he learned to love both classical literature and classical studies – 'such a great gift to have had two wonderful young classics teachers' – and from there went to Oxford to read Classics, Philosophy and Ancient History.

'I'm not the world's greatest scholar but I jogged along happily enough and then went to Cambridge to do theology, where I met the Professor of New Testament studies, Charlie Moule, the Lady Margaret Professor of Divinity, who was to be a major influence on my life.'

Professor Moule ran a Tuesday evening seminar for undergraduates in his rooms, which Dr Carr joined. He learned more New Testament on those Tuesday evenings, he says, than anywhere else in his life, and came to love that part of the work. 'Charlie Moule himself was a great scholar and a very precise one. He made us pay very very close attention to the words in Greek, in particular to the little words: it's the prepositions and conjunctions that actually make the meaning. I well remember an illuminating moment. It was a passage from Romans chapter 8, that strange bit about the inarticulate groans in our prayers and the bondage to decay; Paul talks about the whole creation being in bondage to decay. It's a very difficult passage, and it is not quite clear what it means.

'What Charlie did was to point out that it wasn't the decay that mattered, it was the bondage that mattered. The decay was natural and normal and part of the process: it was being able to accept the process of decay and be freed from the bondage to it that enabled people to live life in the spirit. That's the sort of "turning moment" that happened at those seminars. It was simple attention to the text that opened vistas hitherto unnoticed.'

He smiles as he remembers something. 'Funnily enough, by one of those strange coincidences, when I was first at Westminster I had decided at the 6.30 pm service, where I just talk off the cuff to people, to talk about Romans 8 and bondage to decay, and there was Charlie Moule, sitting in the front row. A friend had brought him without telling me. It made me sort of check my mind as to whether I'd got it right, but fortunately I had.'

Something else Professor Moule did was to bring visiting scholars to the Tuesday evening seminars, which was how Dr Carr met Jürgen Moltmann. 'He later wrote *The Crucified God*, which was one of those life-changing books. When I came to read the book it was very heartwarming to know that I had met him. I didn't really fully understand him in the seminar. I don't really understand him fully in the book but neverthless it is wonderful to discover that the scholars are human beings: in a seminar they can say 'I don't know', in a way they often can't in a book.'

Jürgen Moltmann was not the only great scholar whom Dr Carr met while still a young man. After graduating from Oxford and Cambridge he spent six months at Bossey in Switzerland, with the World Council of Churches. It was a very important period in his life, and also in the life of the Roman Catholic Church: it was the time of the end of Vatican II.

'The great men, like Rahner, Congar and Schillebeeckx, all the great men who'd been silenced, and were now free to speak, came back through Geneva on their way north, and they stopped and talked to us. It was a very memorable time.' And not only because of the visitors: in that year, 1967, for the first time the graduate school at Bossey was attended by members of the Roman Catholic Church. There were 'about seventeen nations and twenty-something denominations represented, or perhaps the other way round, I forget, but we were a large mix anyway.

'We took turns at taking the liturgy: one week it would be Lutheran, another week Baptist, another week Anglican and everybody went to everything ... There were six Roman Catholics. I shall never forget this. They went to the archbishop of Geneva and asked if they could give the rest of us Communion, if they could have a special dispensation to do that, because of the ecumenical nature of the work we were all doing. The archbishop was rather conservative and said no. When they came back from seeing him we had a big struggle about whether they should celebrate Communion with us or not. We all said of course they must because they were a church along with the rest of us, but in the end they didn't.

'I can remember to this day those six Roman Catholics, one a priest, around the altar crying their eyes out during the Communion because the rest of us, the other thirty or so, were all excluded: they couldn't give us Communion. So we were included and excluded at the same time. We were part of the worship, we were their friends, all of us knew the fellowship of the Church, ecumenically, and yet the authority of the Church, or a church, interposed at this point in their lives. To see these six people reduced to tears because the rest of us couldn't take Communion with them – it was a remarkable moment. I think that probably it was quite a contributory factor to my thinking about sacramental aspects of ministry and the Church. I feel very strongly that we as the Church have taken what are essentially natural symbols which belong to everybody – water, oil, wine, bread – and we've privatised them into our own selves and in doing that we've made the sacraments something internal to the life of the Church whereas in actual fact they are on the edge of the Church. If we see the sacraments as first nothing special – everyday bread, wine and water – which become something special in the sacraments of Eucharist and Baptism, we have a natural meeting point. Baptism, for example, can be interpreted for people who come with their child by the natural symbol of water in all its richness: you don't have to begin with the (probably unfamiliar) gospel: you move towards it from what everyone knows about water.'

After the degree in theology at Cambridge Dr Carr was ordained to Luton parish church. When I ask about his decision, if decision is the right word, to seek ordination, he replies that he has to go back a bit to explain that, to when he was around fourteen, which was when he decided he wanted to become a priest. 'I went to a church where quite a lot of ordinands were produced and it seemed to me a good calling. I've never really thought about doing anything else, other than becoming a barrister, so it's something to do with talking, arguing I suppose. I've never really doubted it very much. Of course you have the odd evening when you want to kick the cat, when you wonder what you're doing, but that applies to any job I think.'

He had 'a whale of a time' in Luton, he says, but wasn't there for long because he was soon invited back to Cambridge to teach New Testament studies. He was there for a couple of years before going to do a fellowship in biblical studies at Sheffield University. There he completed a PhD. At that point he was at something of a loose end, looking round for a job but unsure whether he wanted to go back to parochial ministry or return to academic work. Then someone mentioned a centre for research and training that was being developed at Chelmsford Cathedral. He liked the sound of it so went to see Canon Dick Herrick who was in charge of the centre. 'We got on quite well and he asked me to go and see a Dr Pierre Turquet at the Tavistock Institute of Human Relations. Dr Turquet was a consultant to the centre at Chelmsford.

'So I went to see him, and he asked me what I thought about the Roman poets of the silver age. I wondered what on earth we were doing, talking about that but anyway we had a good discussion.'

He learned later that as well as being consultant to the project at Chelmsford Cathedral Dr Turquet was also a very good friend of Canon Herrick. 'Dr Turquet must have said that I would "do" and so I went to Chelmsford.' And almost the first thing that happened was that he was sent to a group relations conference. Group relations work was to be, with theology, a critical discipline in his life for the next thirty years. Based in the psychoanalytic tradition, it has to do with the workings of the conscious and the unconscious in groups. Dr Carr became well known both in America and Europe, amongst secular and religious organisations, for his work in this field. It was this model he was using when we met at the conference in Farnham in 1982.

'It enables one to take seriously what people say both by listening carefully and by giving attention to the affect (or feelings) which they communicate. At Farnham, for example, the almost inevitable contrariness over the blunt question to professionally religious chaplains, "Why pray?", was interpreted rather than, as would happen in society or a study group, politely ignored.

'It struck me that this offered a very useful interpretative model for thinking theologically about the Church, with the advantage of being able to do that in consultation with people and institutions. I, with various colleagues, worked on individual and organisational consultations.'

When he realised that neither Dr Turquet nor Canon Herrick wrote much about the method he began to write about the application of this group relations method to parish ministry and to the Church. 'They were very nervous about fixing the spontaneity of the "here and now" so that it might become a "there and then". It would more than likely then be used as a means of avoiding their own "here and now". But it was abundantly clear that unless some people made the attempt to write about this approach, few people would know anything about it. So I started to write at that point.'

His first book, *The Priestlike Task*, was published in 1985 and in *The Pastor as Theologian* (1989) he shows how the various dynamics that operate in groups correspond to basic Christian theological ideas, and then goes on to demonstrate how these ideas can be used to illuminate not only pastoral ministry to the parish and to people, but also the internal spiritual and theological development of the

Church. He has written eight books in all on this subject.

Dr Carr is careful to emphasise the importance of context in this work. 'Whether you are doing pastoral care and counselling with an individual or consultation with a group such as, perhaps, a bishop's staff, you have to remember the context. Often you find that people are thinking in terms of the managerial context; they've forgotten the psychological context, the empathetic context.

'Another thing about this whole approach is that it brings you back to reality all the time. I well remember consulting to a vicar who had gone to a village where nobody came to his first Easter service. He wondered what on earth had happened to him, so he asked me to go and talk to him, which I did. It suddenly struck me that we should go and look at the register and see if anybody ever had come to the Easter service. And sure enough, nobody ever had come because for some curious reason to do with tradition, with the history of the place, everybody always went off to the church in the next village for the Easter service. So he hadn't done anything wrong at all. Often a simple thing like that can release an enormous amount of energy for ministry which otherwise would be expended on anxiety.'

Dr Carr was made Dean of Bristol in 1987 and was delighted to be there for the ordination of the first women in 1994. 'It's the only time I have had to stop the Peace. After nine minutes I announced that we were going to sing a hymn; it could have gone on forever. It was a wonderful moment.'

In 1997 he moved to London to become Dean of Westminster Abbey. 'So my whole ministry in the end has been educational and three cathedrals – essentially the abbey is like a cathedral – all of which I've enjoyed enormously.'

Looking back he has realised that the group relations

work was especially important for him because it helped him have a greater understanding of the Church without being hidebound by its traditions. 'Over time I developed an enormous – but not uncritical, I hope – admiration for the parochial system and our basic set up, which seems to me a much better device for engaging with people than we realise. We spend all our time stopping the parochial system doing the very thing it does best, which is that it makes available opportunities for people to encounter God. With all its weaknesses the parochial system actually does do that in a rather remarkable fashion. I've become very attached to that aspect of Anglicanism.'

He's also noticed something very interesting over the years, he says, about psychologists, psychotherapists and psychiatrists. When he first began to get to know some of them through his connection with the Tavistock, they were still 'pretty enclosed. They kept fairly strictly within the confines of their own discipline. The boundaries were reasonably clear. Religion, faith and so on were outside those boundaries. But more and more of them in recent years have talked to me about how in the process of counselling or analysing people they seem to reach a point where it goes beyond what they're capable of dealing with. And they begin to use the word "spirituality" which is a very dangerous word because it can mean anything and nothing. We had an inspection recently of one of the schools where I'm involved. The inspector said the school was "marvellous" but that the only thing he was a little worried about was the "spirituality". All of us governors then had a massive discussion about spirituality but we still didn't know precisely what he meant. I think people use that word when they don't know what they mean, because they are going over into an area which they somehow can't totally deal with. A Christian theologian might well say that when you reach that point in your pilgrimage you actually can't say anything. It doesn't matter whether you're some great saint or other or whether you're just a terrible sinner. You hit a point where you are still, quite still, in the presence of God and you are reduced to silence.

'It seems to me that the work of the Church is always in this area of people's experience, bearing in mind that many of them do not care to admit it. Yet among the many boundaries on which the Church operates is that between heaven and earth, which I take to be not between now and hereafter so much as between two perspectives, the earthly and the heavenly, on the same material – namely people's lives, whether as individuals or as groups in society. The word used is 'transcendental', not just because God transcends the world but because the work of the Church transcends, that is lies beyond, normal everyday experience, although naturally remaining fully in touch with it. You see the world with a transcendent reference. Now many, possibly most, people, cannot stand that: it is asking too much. So on their behalf the Church holds that perspective which from time to time becomes necessary in everyday life – for example, at a time of disaster or tragedy. The Church can over-interpret and be too sure about such minimal and confused faith; people then feel rejected and even affronted. Alternatively it can try to work with it, not just for the individual but also, often liturgically, for a larger group or even, as we find at Westminster Abbey, the nation.'

At the end of our talk Dr Carr took me into Westminster Abbey. He didn't say much but his deep affection for the abbey was clear to see. Before leaving for his next appointment he introduced me to a marshal who would help me with any information I wanted or show me round if I wished. There were visitors everywhere and I asked if there were somewhere I could just be quiet. With an understanding nod the marshal led me to the door of the small chapel of St Faith, in the centre of the abbey. I sat down in the stillness. And very soon tears came. Why I was so moved I didn't know; but I did know I felt happy and safe.

Chapter 4

Greece, again

'Fancy a beer?' Ed looks at me, knowing it isn't a question. We are on holiday on the Greek island of Zakynthos, it's early evening and we are strolling along the beach of the great bay of Laganas in the south of the island. We thought we'd left 'civilisation' behind a few hundred yards ago but now we are standing on the sand outside a ramshackle beach bar, open on all three sides, with flapping tarpaulin for a roof, a gravel floor and a scatter of metal topped tables. A row of pink oleanders is the only 'wall' in sight.

What's stopped us is the music. It's vintage Stones, real rhythm and bluesy, something I can't put a name to.

'Yeah, a beer would be nice.'

Ed heads for the bar, eager, not so much for the beer as the prospect of company. He may just be the world's most extraverted extravert. I don't know: I haven't met all of them but I would bet he would be in the top 100, maybe even the top ten. I, on the other hand, would rather have gone to an island without an airport which would have been quieter, and would have chosen to stay at a cottage on a deserted beach rather than in a hotel at the biggest resort on this island. However, when one of the world's greatest extraverts is married to a true introvert, compromises become a way of life. I chose Laganas on Zakynthos because it had a, i.e. *one* disco and a couple of bars but was otherwise pretty, quiet and unspoiled. This is 1985.

The atmosphere at the Driftwood, which turns out to be the name of the bar, is anarchic, hippyish, and veers happily between laid back and manic. But even when it is manic there is nothing forced. Before three days have passed the part owner of the bar, David (his brother Antony is away doing his national service but is expected back any day) asks if we'd like to go to dinner at a local taverna. The owner has told him he has the chance to buy a huge sword-fish but needs to know enough people will come and eat it. We agree. By this time we have met Fiona, from Oxford, an old family friend of David's, whose mother it turns out, is Welsh (hence the 'David').

After several drinks before dinner we go to the taverna. When the swordfish is brought out for us to admire, David plucks out one of its eyes and munches it. Fiona turns pale and I rush her to the loo. She's OK, I'm only OK myself because I shut my eyes. Yuk!

By the end of the holiday I am amazed to find that here at least I can feel comfortable in a group of people. Maybe it's because no one makes me talk or tries to 'include' me; nobody cares if I sit at the edge of the group or out of it on my own, watching the sunset. Nobody bothers me but nobody excludes me. So I'm quiet, maybe the only intro-vert on the island, but who cares. That's fine. It's fine with me, and with everybody else.

We are really looking forward to meeting David's brother. When he comes back there's to be a big party celebrating the end of his national service. We don't, however, get to meet him until the following May. He didn't make it back when he was expected to: his own celebrations in Athens went on a little too long …

We get to know Antony and David and their family well over the years that follow. On one holiday I overhear a conversation between Antony and an English tourist at the bar. Apparently someone had been a little short or maybe even rude to the customer. He and Antony are having a drink together and talking about this. The man is saying he doesn't want to make a fuss, he shrugs it off.

'No', says Antony, gently but firmly, 'no. When you allow someone to speak to you like that, you water down, you dilute, the wine of the human spirit.' And he gives that typical Greek downward inclination of the head to the left which affirms that what he is saying is certainly and importantly true.

Not only had I not expected to hear anyone speaking of the human spirit in the middle of happy hour at the Driftwood, I had had Antony down as an extravert of Edward-type proportions. So I've learned something else: that I have a tendency to categorise people and places too quickly, and that I shouldn't do it, 1) because it strikes me now as being rather a smug thing to do and 2) because I'm probably going to be wrong anyway.

It's while in Greece, in Crete in 1994, this time, that I discover I am a Quaker. I say discover because that is how it happened. There I am, sitting on the beach, with, improbably, a line of ducks quacking past towards the freshwater stream that runs into the sea, when the realisation dawns that I am a Quaker. The decision to become a member of the Society of Friends, to formally apply for membership, has been made while I wasn't looking. How unlikely, but how right that this should happen when I am in Greece, on the beach and not in meeting, not praying, not thinking, just lying around enjoying doing nothing but staring at the sea, the sky and the mountains.

Chapter 5

God of surprises

And then Pilate asked Jesus: 'Are you the king of the Jews?' And Jesus, replied: 'It is you who say it.' Now, what in effect Christ was doing here was asking Pilate if he had asked that question because he truly wanted to know the answer, or because someone else had told him to.[1]

What? I am in the middle of organising my work for the day: as always there's plenty of it. But I stop now, with my pen above my desk diary, and look across at the radio, sitting at the end of my desk, over by the window. I never have the radio on in my office; once in here I am supposed to be working, but it *is* Good Friday and even though I am a Quaker now and Quakers don't have holy days because every day is holy, I still feel I ought to 'do' something to mark Good Friday. Hence the service on the radio.

I continue to go over what the speaker has just said, to turn it round and round in my mind. Could it possibly have anything to do with my own struggle, begun years ago in my teens, about whether to make myself 'accept' the teachings of the Roman Catholic Church, or ask my own questions, go my own way?

[1] Gerard W. Hughes, Friday Service, BBC Radio 4, 1995

The beginning of my decision to leave had been as a result of problems I'd had with the Pope making all my decisions about faith and morality for me, the teaching on original sin, and the teaching on mortal sinfulness, particularly in connection with failure to attend Mass on a Sunday, the eating of meat on a Friday and, last but never least, sex. In short there were some things which I didn't believe that they said I *had* to believe. And what did that mean, I had asked myself, what did it mean to *have to* believe something?

The speaker's words are touching something to do with all this at a very deep level within me. It couldn't be (could it?) that what I had done, years ago, in leaving the Church, was what Christ would have wanted me to do? Would have urged me to do? No. It can't be. I must be mishearing, deluding myself. This is just the very worst kind of self-serving wishful thinking. But I can't pull my mind away from the thought. What if? Just imagine that after all this time of being afraid in case I was wrong, of feeling damned for leaving the Church, I could really believe that far from having committed a mortal sin I had done the right thing? Could it be that staying would have been wrong? Now there's a new thought! But no, that just can't be true. How could leaving possibly be what God would have wanted me to do? I shake my head. No, it can't be, it's just too big a leap. Too absolutely good to be true. The best I can hope for is that He might be neutrally understanding. But what if I'd been wrong, what if it really was a mortal sin? And I'm back once again on the old exhausting seesaw of what if this but what if that. I never seem to be able to resolve it, never seem finally to be able to get rid of the fear of being wrong.

And then as usual, fast to follow on from these thoughts comes the memory of my Dad's early death at the age of fifty-eight. That had been five years after he learned of my doubts about the Church and his health collapsed. Five years after my GP had told me, my Dad having been rushed to hospital following a really frightening asthmatic attack, that unless I recanted he would not be responsible for my father's expectation of life. Dad's health never really recovered and I knew that without the trauma I had inflicted on him he would have lived a much longer life.

And then, again, as usual, comes the next accusation. Some years after my Dad's death I married a man who had been divorced. I was no longer a practising Catholic but you don't cut the ties easily, the imprint of the teaching remains: there is no such thing as divorce. I had left the Church, I had caused, at the very least, great pain and suffering, to my Dad and my Mum, and now, according to the Church's teaching, I was living in sin. How much did I want to cut myself off from God? Was there any more I could do to ensure that I had put myself totally out of reach of His love? I had *chosen*, if the teaching was right, to cut myself off: prayer was useless while I was in this state.

In a bid to seek reassurance that perhaps I had been right and to separate myself completely from the Church, and from the title 'lapsed Catholic', I had become a member of the Church of England. There, I remember thinking at the time: that should make everything all right now. But for some reason it hadn't.

So I had continued looking for some escape from this pressure of fear and apprehension: I did not want to die in mortal terror. In November 1994, after attending Quaker meeting for worship for four years, I became a Quaker. I had long since ceased to believe I could ever conquer the fear completely but I watched myself cautiously to see how much this might help. And it did help but I wasn't surprised to find that there were still times when the fear came back.

Over the years an unwelcome secret prayer, if you could

call it that, had eventually shaped itself into words. A prayer of which I am deeply ashamed; ashamed because it reveals that my fear, cowardice and deference are still alive. The prayer is that a Roman Catholic priest – who, I know very well, I shouldn't need to tell me this – will, nevertheless, tell me that I am not damned for leaving the Church and seeking my own way. This is, of course, an impossible, a logically impossible, prayer, which therefore not even God can answer (if, of course, He is even listening to me) because a Roman Catholic priest would never say that.

And now, in the spring of 1995, as I listen to this Good Friday service, along with all the old fear I am troubled anew, troubled by a quite specific guilt. I shouldn't be here listening to the radio; I should be up in Hindley in Lancashire, where I'm from, and where my mother has been taken into hospital for tests. I remind myself repeatedly that it is only for tests, that I ring her every day and she sounds fine, even chirpy, and that the nurse has suggested I go up a couple of days after Easter when they will have the results. But it's all thin, transparent cant, designed to ease my conscience. Totally ineffective. My conscience is more than pricking; it is giving me no rest at all.

Mum had been to stay with us for a few days last weekend, before, as we then thought, having to go home for her outpatients appointment for tests on the Monday. She had looked terrible, as frail and fragile as a baby bird, all white skin and sharp bones. She is eighty-three years old. She has been a widow for twenty-seven years. She has lived alone for twenty-seven years. I am her only child. Her health and her short-term memory have been deteriorating for several years now. I know I should be there, should have gone without thinking; instinctively. What daughter wouldn't? What proper daughter wouldn't? But somehow I just cannot face it, cannot make myself do it.

And so I properly condemn myself. But still I have chosen not to go: it is Good Friday and here I am at my desk, not at her home in Hindley, getting ready to go and see her at afternoon visiting. When all the other people will have visitors. But not my Mum. Unless one or two of her friends make the effort to get from Hindley to Leigh by bus on a Good Friday – some hope – she will be alone while others chat with their husbands, brothers, sisters, sons and daughters.

I pull my mind back to the radio. When the service ends I learn that the speaker's name is Gerard Hughes. I turn off the radio and get on with my work. Two weeks after Easter Sunday my mother dies.

After her death, after her funeral, when I am home again, back at work in my office, I decide it's time for a bit of a clear up, time to clear my desk. It might help me get down to work, which I'm finding difficult, because I am tired all the time.

I am just about to throw yet another stray piece of paper into the waste paper basket when something written in one corner catches my eye. My handwriting is so bad I can hardly read it. Looks like a name. Gerard Hughes. And there's something else written next to it. God of Surprises. I frown. What's that? Must be a book. And the name ... wasn't that the name of the man on the radio, on Good Friday? I check my diary. Yes, it was. But there'd been no mention of a book. Oh well, here it is. Perhaps I'll get it from the library. I begin to read it on 9 May.

'I am a Catholic, a priest and a Jesuit.'[2]

Oh my God, he's not only a Catholic, he's a priest and he's not only a priest, he's a Jesuit. The strictest kind of Roman Catholic priest there is: the Pope's shock troops! Have I

---

[2] Gerard W. Hughes, *God of Surprises* (Darton, Longman and Todd, 1985), p. ix.

made an awful mistake? Perhaps it would be safer not to read this book? What if it plunges me back into the middle of all my old fears of hell fire for all eternity, what if it rekindles them all over again after I've struggled to quell them for so many years? And I am better than I used to be, I am: I can't go back to how it was, I can't.

I close the book and look at the back cover: it's recommended by Gerald Priestland, author of *Priestland's Progress*, former BBC religious affairs correspondent and a Quaker. He says it's a 'lovely, wise and lucid book of deep humanity'. And I remember the way Gerard Hughes spoke on the radio: his voice had been so normal and everyday, so unpious, and completely lacking in any sort of bullshit or cant. I re-open the book.

> I am a Catholic, a priest and a Jesuit. Many people still think that Catholic priests, perhaps Jesuits especially, never suffer confusion, bewilderment or disillusion. I do.[3]

> When we try to pray, we must have some idea of God in our minds, and this idea will influence how we pray and whether we pray. As a University chaplain I used to spend much time listening to people who had either given up their Catholic faith, or were thinking of doing so, or they were worried about their own honesty in continuing as Catholics when they felt they no longer really believed in the teachings of the Catholic Church. Having listened to them, I always tried to encourage them to speak about their own understanding of God. After many conversations, an identikit image of God formed in my imagination.

[3] ibid.

God was a family relative, much admired by Mum and Dad, who described him as very loving, a great friend of the family, very powerful and interested in all of us. Eventually we are taken to visit 'Good Old Uncle George'. He lives in a formidable mansion, is bearded, gruff and threatening. We cannot share our parents' professed admiration for this jewel in the family. At the end of the visit, Uncle George turns to address us.

'Now listen, dear,' he begins, looking very severe, 'I want to see you here once a week, and if you fail to come, let me just show you what will happen to you.' He then leads us down to the mansion's basement. It is dark, becomes hotter and hotter as we descend, and we begin to hear unearthly screams. In the basement there are steel doors. Uncle George opens one.

'Now look there, dear,' he says. We see a nightmare vision, an array of blazing furnaces with little demons in attendance, who hurl into the blaze those men, women and children who failed to visit Uncle George or to act in a way he approved.

'And if you don't visit me, dear, that is where you will most certainly go,' says Uncle George. He then takes us upstairs again to meet Mum and Dad. As we go home, tightly clutching Dad with one hand and Mum with the other, Mum leans over us and says, 'And now don't you love Uncle George with all your heart and soul, mind and strength?' And we, loathing the monster, say, 'Yes, I do,' because to say anything else would be to join the queue at the furnace. At a tender age religious schizophrenia has set in and we keep telling Uncle George how much we love him and how good he is and that we want to do only what pleases him. We observe what we are told are his wishes and dare not admit, even to ourselves, that we loathe him.

Uncle George is a caricature, but a caricature of a truth, the truth that we can construct a God who is an image of our tyrannical selves. Hell-fire sermons are out of fashion, but they were in fashion a few decades ago and they may well come in again. Such sermons have a great appeal to certain unhealthy types of mind, but they cause havoc with the more healthy and sensitive.[4]

The danger in the institutional element in religion is that we never advance beyond a religious infantilism. We attend religious services, hear sermons and religious instructions, are told what is, and what is not, the Church's moral and doctrinal teaching, and the danger is that we may be content with this and desire to go no further ... There is also the danger for those in authority in the Churches that they may encourage people to remain in the infantile state, calling this retarded state 'being humble, loyal, faithful and observant' and threatening with the wrath of God anyone who dares to disagree. There is no more effective way of destroying true faith in God than by misusing words like loyalty, humility, obedience and faithfulness. These are important virtues which can help us to keep true and attentive to the promptings of God at work within us, but to use these virtues for the opposite purpose, namely to destroy any belief that God does work within our minds and hearts by assuring people that any disagreement with religious authorities must stem from their own sinfulness, so

[4] ibid., p. 34.

discouraging them from paying any attention to their own inner experience, the place of their encounter with God, is a sin and a scandal, and Christ has harsh words to say of those who scandalise children: 'It were better that a millstone were hung around their neck and they were thrown into the sea'.[5]

For Catholics, quite apart from the major crimes which would bring a life-sentence in any respectable criminal court, there are many other acts and omissions which can incur an eternal sentence in conditions which would make the Gulag Archipelago seem like a luxury hotel in comparison. Deliberately missing Mass on Sunday or 'wilful pleasure in the irregular motions of the flesh' brought the same penalty as torture and mass murder ... The damage done to a sensitive and imaginative person by this kind of teaching is tragic and a perversion of the Good News.

Having listened to one particular person who had suffered inner torture through this kind of teaching, I was not at all surprised when, in answer to my question, 'If you were completely free of all moral obligations, what would you most like to do?', she answered, 'Burn down churches.'[6]

One night when he was 'about two and a bit', Gerard Hughes recalls, as he was being put to bed by his older sister, Marie, he sat on the edge of the bed and said the word 'God'. He wanted to see what would happen. Now, seventy-odd years later, this scene of himself sitting on the bed, facing the window, is clear and sharp in his mind. But

[5] ibid., p. 19.
[6] ibid., p. 66.

for many years this memory was completely lost to him. 'Of course it's only with hindsight, when you look back, and reflect, that you begin to see, to sift out some memories from others.'

When he was five the family moved from Skelmorlie in the Scottish countryside to Glasgow. Although he didn't know why at the time, it was because his father was ill, and, with six children of school age to support, his mother needed to return to work teaching music. His father died of pneumonia three years later.

In Glasgow they lived in a tenement chosen because it was near the Jesuit Church and College of St Aloysius and the Convent School of the Sisters of Mercy. Gerard went to the St Aloysius primary school and from there, at the age of thirteen, to the Jesuit boarding school of Mount St Mary's, in Sheffield, where his brother Ian had been.

The school offered a scholarship to pupils in their school certificate year which meant their school fees would be paid for the next two years. The sixteen-year-old Gerard decided it was worth giving it a try. He grins. 'So I did a bit of extra study and then, to top up the study, I thought "a bit of prayer". Which meant that occasionally I would go into chapel and recite prayers. That was my way of praying then, and I thought, you know, that should help a bit with the scholarship.'

He didn't get the scholarship but he did discover something. In between 'babbling' the strings of Our Fathers and Hail Marys aimed at improving his chances of getting the scholarship, he sometimes remained silent and simply knelt in the chapel. And a different kind of praying became apparent to him and with it came 'a strange attractiveness'. He can't explain what happened during those moments of non-babbling prayer in chapel. 'There was just this mysterious attractiveness ... it wasn't a sort of "flashing light experience" that gave me certainty.' There was no feeling of certainty, he says, but there was the beginning of an awareness of something different from anything he'd experienced before: 'this mysterious attractiveness of God'. There was a feeling, albeit 'extremely vague', that what he was doing was 'somehow the right sort of thing to do'.

He didn't make any connections at the time but has realised since – yet another instance of reflective hindsight – that it was at about this time that he began to think about becoming a priest. And one evening two years later, back in Skelmorlie for their summer holidays, he was listening to music and gazing at 'a most beautiful sunset over the Firth of Clyde. I knew then that I had to become a Jesuit. While part of me was repelled by the thought, at another level I knew this was what I must do.'

After two years in the Jesuit noviceship, and a further two years of 'the juniorate training' at the Jesuit house of St Beuno's in North Wales, three years of philosophy at Heythrop, the Jesuit College (then based in the Cotswolds), and two years of teaching at Stonyhurst College, a Roman Catholic boarding school for boys in Lancashire, he was sent to Oxford to study Classics. For the first time since the age of five he was being taught by people who were neither Jesuits nor Roman Catholics, and had as fellow students men and women who either had little interest in religion or were puzzled by the whole idea of religious life. Wearing his then compulsory uniform of black suit and Roman collar he felt at first like 'a stranger from outer space', but was more at ease on the afternoons when, 'collarless' he played rugby or squash.

He was greatly struck by the intelligence, courtesy and patience of his tutors in Greek and Latin prose and deeply affected by the way they taught. They encouraged him; there was no emphasis on mistakes and shortcomings.

Likewise, the way his philosophy tutors taught came as something of a revelation, in that they actively encouraged him to think for himself and to trust his own judgement.

It was another twenty years before he realised that this Oxford method of teaching was, in fact, closer to the principles of the Spiritual Exercises of Ignatius of Loyola, founder of the Jesuits, than Heythrop's teaching methods. 'If we are not encouraged to think for ourselves, then we are likely to find a ready-made God, a God of convention, not the God of life who constantly calls us out of our own handed-down, fixed way of thinking to a sense of wonder, and to freedom.'

What happened at the time, however, because of his tutors and some of the friends he made through rugby and squash, was that he asked himself the question: how it was that such gifted, good and intelligent men couldn't see the obvious truth of Roman Catholicism? He had always been taught to pray for the conversion of Britain, and of course Russia, home to the twin evils of atheism and communism, but now he added his friends and tutors to the list.

He remembers walking in the college grounds one evening during a summer vacation, when, suddenly, a thought came to him. '"Is the whole thing a cod?" You know, the Christianity thing.' He smiles to himself now, remembering. 'I know partly where this thought came from. It was from one of the books I had to read, which was by a gentleman called Lucretius, a Latin poet, whose vocation in life was to rid people of religion. He thought religion was the source of all evil because religion engenders fear and fear destroys people.

'It was a curious experience ... obviously when you study philosophy you think "Is there a God? Is there not a God?", you examine the proofs for the existence of God, etc.; but nothing of that ever touched me. This moment did touch me. It was like being hurled into an abyss and there was just nowhere to stand. And I thought – because of the religious teaching I had had – "This is temptation, pray against it." So I prayed like blazes for faith. But I couldn't look at this doubt, it was far too dangerous. It was only years later, with hindsight, that I realised how important that moment was. It was an invitation to review my notions of God ... but it was just too overwhelming. It touched me at a level at which I had no recollection of being touched before.'

He pauses.

'And again, with hindsight, I can see that the process went on. I couldn't stop the questioning. And the questioning was extremely fruitful.'

But did he go with the questioning at the time, as it were, pursue it, or did he try to stop it?

'Oh no, I tried to stop it. I just thought, "That's a temptation, get on with your work." I didn't realise it was an invitation to look at my ideas of God and to move from a belief in a threatening and remote God to belief in a God "closer to me than I am to myself". Because I interpreted the experience as a temptation, it was an invitation I didn't accept.'

After Oxford came a year of theology at Heythrop, then three years of theology in Germany where he was ordained and where he came across the writings of Karl Rahner, 'probably the most outstanding theologian of the twentieth century'. Karl Rahner, who, like Gerard, was a Jesuit, was asking questions about what was meant by 'grace', about the relationship between the natural and the supernatural life and about the essential nature of the Church. He had also given a series of lectures on the Spiritual Exercises of St Ignatius.

'Rahner's writings and his questioning resonated very

deeply within me.' In the 1960s, when he was once again teaching at Stonyhurst, these resonances began to break through into his mind in the form of disturbing questions about how what he believed was reflected in his life, in the life of the Church, and in the life of the school. It was the practice at Stonyhurst for the boys to stay on until Easter Monday when Easter fell early. On Easter Sunday, following 'all the Holy Week services which were in those days extremely long, elaborate and severe, the Feast of the Resurrection was celebrated by Mass followed by a military parade. Apart from all the Holy Week services, the boys spent most of the week polishing their buttons and preparing their kit for the march-past in front of the rector, who took the salute standing on a specially-erected dais.'

One particular Easter Sunday, Gerard was up early and was met in the playground by a near-apoplectic colonel, who was in charge of the combined cadet force. The enraged colonel led him to a large wall on which someone had painted the nuclear disarmament symbol and beneath it 'March begins here. (No children please.)' The rector's dais had disappeared overnight and was now floating on one of the college's large ornamental ponds.

Gerard was put 'in charge of criminal investigations' but found he had no heart for the tracking down and the punishment of the culprit. He'd a good idea who had done it: a boy in the sixth form, Eric Kemmet, known to his class as 'the atheist', and a pupil in one of Gerard's religious education classes. 'I had a great liking for Eric. He was a very bright lad and showed very great attention in RE classes, whereas the true believers slept their way through them. We kept in touch after he left ... He died young. I conducted his Requiem Mass. His wife asked me ... He was an honest inquirer; an honest inquirer ... And what he, and some other "atheist/agnostic" pupils at Stonyhurst taught me was that it's the questioners who are more open to truth, and therefore to God, rather than those who accept what they are taught but aren't interested enough to question.'

And as the perpetrator of the Easter Sunday prank, Eric had another lesson for him, in the form of a question, which bred yet other questions. The question that Eric's prank brought into his mind was: 'Is it not a greater offence to encourage children to celebrate the Feast of the Resurrection with the weaponry of death than for a child to play a prank like Eric had done?

'Now, that triggered off God knows how many questions. Not just the peace issue but what is the nature of God; what are the real roots of violence; what is the relationship between faith and life; is saving our souls a purely private matter between God and ourselves, etc.? It was a question which has changed the direction of my life.'

He smiles. 'Of course, I didn't see that at the time.'

From Stonyhurst Gerard was sent, in 1967, to be chaplain to Roman Catholic students at Glasgow University. He learned a great deal, he says, from the students and also from the other people, whom he met at Glasgow, and while there was twice dismissed from his post and reinstated. The first dismissal followed a letter he wrote to his archbishop about his theological and philosophical difficulties with the recently promulgated papal encyclical, *Humanae Vitae*, which declared contraception to be intrinsically wrong in all imaginable circumstances.

'I didn't reject the encyclical; I simply wanted to tell him about my problems with it. I believed in the openness of the Church, especially following Vatican II; this was something to be open about or, God help us, so I thought.' And he chuckles, shaking his head at his own naivety.

The archbishop wrote back to express his astonishment that a Jesuit could possibly doubt a papal encyclical and three weeks later he got the news that he was to leave his post as chaplain after Christmas – he'd written to the archbishop in October. And he was to tell nobody about it, not to say a word.

'I just felt, well, hit on the head. I mean I knew theoretically that the Church is a sinful Church, that there is corruption in the Church, etc but ... I was naive. I did not think this was possible.' But strangely, a reprieve followed fairly swiftly and once again he was told to say nothing about it. That was in 1968. In 1972 he heard again from the archbishop that he was to leave the chaplaincy with no reasons given.

'This time there was a hell of a kerfuffle and eventually it hit the press. I remember one moment, in the middle of the crisis. I was going out to say Mass and I had to tell the congregation that I'd been sacked, and I thought "Well, maybe I am in the wrong place, maybe I should just go." I was really feeling low. And, somehow, in the course of the Mass I sensed, just momentarily, that it was all right, that I must hold by what I believed. It was a sense of God being with me, which I found extraordinarily helpful. But, you know, when God says "I'm with you", that doesn't mean God can't leave you in an awful situation when you feel as though there's nobody there ... But there was just that moment, when I could just think that it was going to be all right, that it wasn't disastrous.'

A reprieve followed once again, but it was not until the present archbishop had left and another appointed that Gerard learned what had been behind his second dismissal. 'The reasons were that I had given Holy Communion to Protestants and that I had questioned whether there should be Catholic schools.

'Now neither of those questions were put to me. And I just thought "I can't believe this sort of behaviour is happening in the Church, that there can be these sort of forces, where you are not allowed to speak, that you are kept quiet." And all of a sudden I was thinking "Where is the freedom of the children of God, where is the truth of it?"'

Although it was an awful time for him, he can see now that those experiences forced him to think hard about allegiance to a Church, to an institution. 'We can become so devoted to a system — and it's a constant danger in all religions — that it can, as it were, take away our humanity.'

And it was also while he was in Glasgow that he first really became aware of how a certain kind of religious upbringing, what might be called now an old-fashioned Roman Catholic upbringing, can engender a split in our spirituality. This is perhaps best exemplified by a story he tells in *God of Surprises*, about a young woman student who felt guilty about going away to Spain to study. When she told him this Gerard found himself completely baffled, but having recently done a counselling course, instead of saying he didn't understand he simply repeated what she had said. And she went on to say that the reason she felt guilty about going to Spain was because it would mean she didn't have to go to Mass any more and to keep on pretending she was still a Catholic when she wasn't. She only continued to attend Mass, she said, so as not to offend her parents and Roman Catholic relatives and friends. 'She found going to Mass a meaningless bore, and the teachings of the Church, as she understood them, to be statements about a world which had no meaning to her. She wanted to drop the lot and live, but she was not yet strong enough inside to live out her convictions.'

Gerard asked her what she wanted to do when she had finished her Spanish degree and she replied that she wanted to go and teach in Peru where she had heard there was tremendous poverty. She said she felt she had been given so much she wanted to share something of what she had been given with those who had little or nothing.

When he asked if she thought she might have a vocation from God she told him not to be daft!

'She thought of herself as irreligious and unspiritual, yet her dominant emotion was compassion; she wanted to share what she had been given, and in gratitude for what she had received, she wanted to serve.'

From this time on he began to be even more keenly aware of, and more troubled by, something he perceived frequently around him, and in himself, something he began to call 'split spirituality'. Operating on split spirituality meant that you could practise your religion in one compartment as it were, where it was orderly and safe but then on the other hand, over there was 'real' life. It was around this time that he met Stella Reekie, whose spirituality was by no means split. During World War II Stella had been a Red Cross nurse and had been one of the first into Belsen concentration camp. She described this as her 'road to Damascus experience'. She spent the rest of her life helping refugees and the very poor. After working for many years in Pakistan as a Church of Scotland missioner she eventually returned to Glasgow to retire.

At the time Gerard met her, however, despite supposedly being retired, she had been appointed by the joint churches in Glasgow to work with immigrant Asian families. 'She had a small flat near the university, known as the international flat, which was usually crowded with people from India, Pakistan and Africa. If you were invited to a meal there it was advisable to eat immediately because other visitors were bound to arrive and you'd be expected to contribute from your own plate to make a meal for them.

'Stella used to say that whenever I saw her coming I used to run away. It was only partly true. She was always sure to ask you to do something impossible – never for herself, always for somebody else. She was so keen to do things to help other people that she assumed everybody else was of similar virtue, which of course we weren't.

'Poor Stella died of cancer and at her funeral service – the church was packed with people of all nations and faiths, and none – one of the people who gave an address was a Sikh. He compared Stella to water which is life-giving, cleansing, refreshing and assumes the shape of whatever contains it. "Stella", he said, "was to me a Sikh, to my Muslim friends a Muslim, a Hindu to Hindus." He ended by saying that he'd never understood what Christians meant when they said that Jesus died for our sins. "But", he said, "I do know that Stella lived for us."

'I thought that was a wonderful tribute. Stella epitomised what a lot of other people in Glasgow showed me, that God is at work in the hearts of all people, whether they have any faith or none.'

The difficult times with his own church in Glasgow, and what he learned from so many individuals there, has led him, he says, to a vision of the Church 'which is broader, more exciting and inclusive of all people.

'Canon Max Warren, who was a Secretary of the Church Mission Society in Africa, once wrote that whenever you meet another person, "of another faith, or no faith, you should take off your shoes because you are entering sacred ground, and tread warily, because God has been there before you". It's marvellous how somebody can write something and suddenly you think "That's it." That holds so much, that little phrase.'

He discovered another significant phrase when, following his time at Glasgow, and at his own request, he went to Rome to study in more depth the Spiritual Exercises of St Ignatius. He defines the Spiritual Exercises as 'a carefully graded series of Scripture-based passages designed to allow our hidden self to grow strong'. He had 'done' the Exercises, or as he would say now, a 'form of them', during his training as a Jesuit. The Exercises had lasted a month and had involved four lectures a day, followed by prayer focused on those four talks, a daily meeting with one's spiritual director and, in between, silence. It was only after his long training as a Jesuit that he discovered that in Ignatius's time, the Spiritual Exercises were given individually because they were to be adapted to the needs, ability, energy and willingness of the retreatant.

The significant phrase, which struck him so forcefully, described the Spiritual Exercises as being 'suitable for Catholics, for Protestants and for Pagans'. It was written by Jerome Nadal, a contemporary of St Ignatius, and was, says Gerard, 'a revelation'. Here was a sixteenth-century Jesuit, who had been there when Ignatius was first giving the Exercises, and he was saying they were for everybody, for people of all faiths and of none. A further discovery was Ignatius's intention that during the Exercises the pilgrim, as Gerard calls the person doing the Exercises, should pray four times a day and then meet with their spiritual director to talk about what was happening in their prayer, without being subjected to any talks or lectures.

As Gerard knew, this was not how the Exercises were given to Jesuits. And as for ordinary, non-religious people, being able to do these Exercises, individually, as intended, and not in a group as now happened, well that was just unthinkable.

'It's only by doing the Exercises as originally described by Ignatius that one begins to understand what is in fact happening, and in particular what emotions and feelings are coming through. Only in that way does one begin to understand what is going on in us.' So how did

Ignatius's original intentions and instructions get lost?

'Well, the common explanation is that when the Exercises were first given they became so popular that demand exceeded supply, and so they began to be given in groups. But the real reason, I am convinced, is that the method was too threatening to some in the Church. At the time Ignatius was condemned by the theologians of Paris as an illuminist, a form of heretic: that is, someone who says the Holy Spirit works on us or in us directly without the need for intervention by the Church. That was the accusation. Because the Exercises can help people to discover for themselves, to rely more on themselves, to have the courage to speak their minds and to experience the freedom of the children of God, people become less submissive and that can be difficult for those in authority!'

In 1976 Gerard went to Canada to a centre where the Exercises were being given to individuals and people were being trained to give them. Two years later, while working with final year Jesuits back at St Beuno's, he was given permission to set up a centre there for the study and the development of the Spiritual Exercises. He and his colleagues in this difficult-to-organise venture – no staff, no money – wanted to reach people 'of all faiths and of none' and to avoid, at the other extreme, an intake entirely made up of Roman Catholic religious, many of whom were duty bound to make at least one annual retreat.

'Three of us at St Beuno's used to dream of a house open to "Catholics, Protestants and Pagans" where the Spiritual Exercises could be offered individually. To make this possible, we would have to limit the Roman Catholic applicants, so we thought one method might be to award −1 to any retreat given taking a Catholic priest or religious, +1 for a Roman Catholic lay person, +2 for a person of another denomination, and +8 for a card-carrying Communist or a

Roman Catholic bishop. We actually had three Communists before we had a bishop.'

The points system was a joke, a mind game, but it helped to keep them focused on the people to whom they were trying to offer the Exercises.

St Beuno's did eventually become a very successful centre for the Spiritual Exercises. But that was by no means a signal to sit back because very quickly Gerard began to realise that beyond the people who were coming to do the Exercises were many more who simply couldn't find the time and/or the money to come to St Beuno's. What about all of them? How could the Exercises be made available to them? The first answer was to begin to offer three-monthly training courses to people who would themselves then give the Exercises to others beyond St Beuno's.

Some time later, came a second answer. While sitting in a pub one lunchtime with his friend Graham Chadwick (the former Anglican bishop of Kimberley during the years of apartheid, who got kicked out of South Africa 'for asking too many questions') who had himself done the three-month training course at St Beuno's, the two of them decided that, in response to increasing demand, they would put on a two-week course for people with some experience of the Exercises on how to communicate the Exercises to others.

Gerard estimates that since it began, in 1985, at an agricultural college, Llysfasi, in North Wales, about 800 people have completed the two-week course, which is run annually and sometimes twice a year.

Currently he is based at the Jesuit house in Birmingham, specialising in working on spirituality with people involved in peace and justice. Over the years, he says, he has come across many such people. 'Many of them do not consider their work as having anything to do with spirituality, and they are never likely to go anywhere near a "spirituality" course.'

So, I ask, feeling a bit as if I'm asking a 64-million-dollar question: 'What's your definition of spirituality, of the spiritual? What does it mean when someone says they "work in spirituality"?'

'I would say that, speaking as a Christian, spirituality is about the spirit. The spirit is God and what you are talking about is God, and the godliness in every single individual and the goodness in all creation. When you use the words "I work in spirituality" what it means is that you are attempting to become more and more aware of God, closer to all of us than we are to ourselves, the ultimate source of all our desiring.

'And it is wonderful when it does start dawning on people, individually. Seeing it dawning on them is … But it is not something you can teach somebody, it is not something you can do for them. You can be enabling, but it is something a person discovers; it's not a task; it's not something they have to learn. It's already there.

'The Quakers have a lovely phrase: "to discover that of God in everyone" … And if we are not in touch with our own stories, we can't be in touch with God.'

Ah, that reminds me. Speaking of God, he hasn't told me what happened all those years ago when he was two-and-a-bit and he sat on the edge of his bed and said the word: 'God'?

A quick glance at his watch: he's worried that we might miss our lunch, we've been talking for quite a long time.

'Oh', he says, smiling, 'nothing. Nothing happened.'

Chapter 6

Do I dare?

'Hi, Ann. You're keen on *God of Surprises*, aren't you? Didn't you say that a while back?' asks Barbara.

'Yes, yes, I did.'

I've come to know Barbara, and to like her a lot, during the seven or so years I've been coming to Quakers. She's just come up to me as we're having a cuppa after meeting for worship. Meeting was dull and dry for me and it's been that way for a while.

'Right, thought so,' she says. 'Well, there's an eight-day Ignatian retreat at the Anglican convent in Ham next May. You know, like the ones you said Gerard Hughes described in the book.'

The convent is only ten minutes away by bus from where I live in Richmond, in Surrey. I can easily get there. I can do an Ignatian retreat. I am thrilled and afraid all at the same time. Thrilled because I have wanted to do an Ignatian retreat ever since I read *God of Surprises* in 1995 and afraid because it means coming into contact with a Catholic priest, and a Jesuit at that. OK, he'll be giving the retreat along the lines described by Gerard Hughes in *God of Surprises,* but he could still be one of the old school. I don't want to be frightened to death and beyond all over again. I can't risk that. Can I?

I decide at least to find out more and ring the convent, St Michael's, for a programme of events for the coming year.

When it arrives I see that there is a quiet day on Ash Wednesday. Maybe I could go to that and kind of test the waters?

Thinking about the retreat I realise that if I do decide to do it it will be very hard to leave Ed – and Ginger, our cat – for eight days, knowing they'll be just up the road. That will feel very odd. And what about the silence of the retreat: will I be able to go for eight days without speaking? As a Quaker I am keen on silence and crave it if my life gets too noisy and busy. But eight days? For one of the world's great rabbiters? It also crosses my mind as to whether I can get through eight days without a glass of white wine. That'll be a first. Nevertheless I decide to at least sign up for the Ash Wednesday quiet day. Surely I can risk that, can't I? And then I can decide if I dare to enrol for the retreat.

Chapter 7

God of the impossible

'I'm going to put some slips of paper on the table. They each have a sentence written on them. Take the one that you get a reaction to – good or bad. Take it to your room and just contemplate it, focus your thoughts on it.'

The man speaking is a Jesuit priest. His name is Colm. He's dressed in shirt, pullover and corduroys. But he still looks like a Jesuit. He's the person leading the eight-day retreat at St Michael's, which I now know is a convent of the Community of the Sisters of the Church. This is the first evening: we've had a meal and now we're at our short introductory session.

I glance at one of the two nuns who are also leading the retreat, Sister Linda Mary. I wouldn't be here but for Sister Linda Mary. My first visit to the convent had been for the day of prayer and silence on Ash Wednesday, three months ago, which she had led. I hadn't known what to expect. Which was just as well because she said things like: 'An awareness of sin is an awareness of God' and that her own favourite place to die would be under a gum tree in the middle of the Australian outback. She was an Australian nun.

At the end of that day, most uncharacteristically, I had felt sufficiently at ease with her to confide my misgivings about the eight-day Ignatian retreat I was thinking of attending at the convent in May. I knew from the advance information about the retreat that she was one of the people involved in running it. To my complete surprise I had heard myself telling her that I was an ex-Catholic and very nervous about Jesuits. I certainly didn't want to attend the retreat only to have old but still very real fears of eternal damnation stoked up because of my having left the Church. I knew that each person attending the retreat would be appointed a spiritual director and I was fearful of the risk of having a Jesuit as my spiritual director. I just couldn't handle that: apart from anything else I'd be too afraid to be open with him. She'd smiled and said there was no need to worry, and that if I wanted to, since we'd now met and spoken, I could simply write in and ask for her to be my spiritual director on the retreat. Which I had done.

Now here I am at the start of the retreat and hoping fervently that my request hasn't gone astray. We've all just been asked to say why we are here. I don't know what to say and feel I've been put on the spot. My friend Carol says she is looking for some sort of direction in her life. I reckon that will do for me too. It's not the truth but I don't want to reveal to everybody that I've been inspired to attend by Gerard Hughes's book, *God of Surprises*. He has been one of the pioneers of these short Ignatian retreats for lay people 'of all denominations and of none' and that is why I'm here. But this takes me too close to the image of good old Uncle George, and how do I know that this Jesuit is like Gerard Hughes? He might not be. It seems unlikely given the sisters' openness and lack of judgementalism but I can't risk it. So best to keep all that to myself.

I look over the pieces of paper to see if anything 'strikes' me. 'Jesus reached out and touched me' is written on one slip of paper. Yuk! Pass me the sickbag, Susan! Can't stand all this sentimental mush! Well, he did say to choose the one you had a reaction to, so … With a smothered sigh of exasperation I pick up the scrap of paper and go off to my room to 'contemplate'.

I sit in the chair by the window, lean back and close my eyes. Of course I could just fall asleep. It's so quiet here. The only noise is the distant hum of traffic on the road to Kingston. Almost soothing when it's that far away. Hugely reluctant, not wanting to spoil this little moment of peace, and because of the distaste I feel for the words themselves, I bring them before my mind: Jesus reached out and touched me. *(The first time I wrote this I actually wrote 'teached' not 'touched'.)*

Straight away I see a well. A small boy. I am the small boy. I'm about five or six. The ground around the well is muddy, where people have slopped water. It is a sunny day. There are olive trees in the middle distance. I am playing in the clay-like mud by the well. I'm happy and absorbed, enjoying the squidge of the clay as I shape it into a fat little bird. Well it's supposed to be a bird, I think, as I pull out a tiny pointy beak, frowning in concentration, intent on my creation.

Somebody comes up beside me. A stranger. With my bird held in my cupped hands I look up to see who it is. And I see a man, smiling down at me. He reaches out his hand and touches my head very gently. I look up at him properly now, right into his eyes. He's not a stranger. He knows me. He knows me through and through; he's always known me. And he has loved me for the same length of time. He knows me through and through and he loves me the same way. The only thing I can think of to do to say thank you is to hold up to him, as a gift, the clay bird I have made. He accepts it, smiling his thanks, and as he touches it, it spreads its wings and flies away.

And I come back to the room and I am sobbing.

The next morning we do an exercise in which we all write a line of what comes into our heads, pass it on to the next person to do the same, and then it all gets put together. The result, someone says, is poetry. Later on, when people take it in turn to talk about their faith I become irritated to the point of anger. Everybody is so sure, there is not a whisper of doubt or uncertainty. I don't believe it. Have I come to the wrong place? Is this all going to be a waste of time? The session ends. My face set and hard, I march towards the door. But Colm intercepts me. 'So, did you enjoy that?' he asks. The glare of anger is still in my eyes as I reply with the only words I find it possible to say: 'Thank you.' I turn away from him and leave.

A couple of mornings later we do finger-painting.

But I don't *do* finger painting, I think to myself. It's just not me. I can't do this. I don't want to.

Express how you feel inside, we are told: just do what you like. This makes me feel very uncomfortable but I am here, so ... and once I have my first big splotch of blue on the paper I find I am smiling. This is a strange feeling but it's nice. My big swathe of bright blue gets bigger on the white paper. Just blue. After we've had quite some time on our 'painting' Colm tells one half of the room to close their eyes while the other half crosses the room and adds whatever colour they like to their paintings.

When I open my eyes, right in the middle of my swathe of clear blue is a big splodge of bright red.

'How do you feel about that?' Colm asks me.

I grin. 'Well, I'd expected to feel that I wouldn't like any-thing anybody did to my painting, and I really dislike red, but somehow I don't mind.' I pause, trying to find the right words. 'It's livelier now – it's got more energy.' And I go away thinking about red and energy. And anger. Isn't red the colour of anger?

God of the impossible

Anger comes up in my afternoon session with Linda Mary. We have an hour's session with our spiritual director each afternoon: otherwise, ever since the second day, the retreat has been silent. We are talking about my fear when I left the Church. That's still with me, I say, although it's a lot better than it was, particularly since reading *God of Surprises*. She asks if I'm angry about the fear. After a couple of minutes, while I try to understand what she means, I arrive at a realisation that if they'd done this to anybody else I would be burning with rage on behalf of the terrorised person. We talk about being angry, about how we didn't show anger in my family when I was little, except on the one or two occasions when it erupted from my father and I was so scared I never wanted it to happen again. Making him angry was something to be carefully avoided. I couldn't remember my mother ever being angry: it was unthinkable, unimaginable that she would ever have been angry with Dad. What about me being angry? Me? Strange question. I think hard and remember one occasion. I must have been around nine or ten and my best friend had cheated me out of my turn at a game of two-ball against the wall. She was eighteen months older than me: she was always the leader, I was happy to be the follower. Yet this one time I reacted completely differently. I lashed out at her and when she ran away from my fists and my punches, past her Dad who'd come to the door to see what the commotion was, he had to hold me back physically to stop me from chasing after her.

At this point Linda Mary says another of her amazing things: 'Jesus is angrier than you are about what has been done to you.'

I stare at her, my lips parted in disbelief. What? What is she talking about? This is way too much to take in.

'You could express how you feel with your painting?'

she suggests, making it a question for me to consider.

I look out of the window at the pink horse chestnuts moving in the light summer breeze on this sunny May afternoon. And I remember good old Uncle George. And a pure fountain of almost orgasmic anger rises through me, floods me. I could kill good old Uncle George. The bastard. Oh yes, I could certainly kill him. I could mash his pompous face to a bloody pulpy mess. And enjoy it. Oh yes, I could do that. How many years have I been maggotty riddled with fear of him and of hell? How many years of trying to ignore the fear, hide from it? Fear of him. Fear of hell. All those years; from being a child. I was just a little girl when all this started.

'Yes,' I say, slowly, out loud, 'Yes, I could do that.'

She nods and smiles, encouraging me.

At the end of the session I walk to the room where the morning sessions of the retreat are held: all our paintings are laid out on our tables. It is still and empty in the afternoon sunshine. I go over to my table. There is the painting with the splodge of lovely bright bright red at its heart. I take out a thin biro from my pocket. I slash the biro repeatedly across the paper, all my weight behind it, delighting and pressing even harder as the paper tears. Kriss kross, kriss kross, kriss kross. Deep blood-running holes in the body of good old Uncle George. When I stop I am a little out of breath. I've thought for a long time that anger often disguises fear but how strange that it has never occurred to me until now that anger can conquer fear, flood it away: that it can be good, not always to be avoided, not always to be feared.

I walk slowly back to my room, lie down on my bed and fall fast asleep.

God of the impossible

Linda Mary's call to the religious life came when she was seventeen and in a state of despair. She had been very sick with hepatitis, and had struggled through her final school exams by sleeping for three hours, then studying for three hours over the weeks of the study break and the examinations. 'What I was feeling was "What's the use of life, why don't I just go and end it?"'

What she did in fact was to go and see her parish priest. 'He told me there was one person who could help me. He meant God or Jesus and I said "I don't want to have anything to do with him, thank you very much."'

Later that night and, she believes, coming out of the experience of her talk with the parish priest, she received a call from God to the religious life. 'It was as clear as that, like God audibly speaking to me, saying: "I want you to be a sister." And I said: "Well, I guess I'll have to be a Roman Catholic then, won't I, God?", because I didn't know then there were Anglican sisters. But I said, "OK, yes, I'll be a sister." And I went straight to sleep. Next morning I thought, "What have I done?"'

Linda Mary was born in Dubbo, New South Wales, Australia, a wide open part of the country where wheat plains stretch for miles. She was the eldest of five children; their mother sent them to Sunday School from the age of five and when they were confirmed she accompanied them to church.

'So there was that connection with the Church but there was nothing at home, we never said grace or talked about God or anything.'

At school she was, she says, an average student. She took maths, science and home science for her Higher School Certificate and then went to Sydney Teachers Training College to train as a teacher of home science. It was while head of department in a local high school that the second call from God came: the call to become a priest.

'I was driving home from school one afternoon, singing, probably a hymn knowing me, and flat (I have since learned not to sing flat), just driving along and again I could hear God speaking to me, as though with a voice. "I want you to be a priest", God said. And again I responded, "Yes", and if anything with a greater sense of conviction than I had to the call to be a sister, although becoming a priest seemed a complete impossibility at the time. I didn't even know, back then in 1971, that there was a movement for the ordination of women, let alone that women were being ordained.' She pauses for a few seconds before continuing. 'But for me God is the God of the impossible.'

I ask how it is that, since she heard the call to become a sister so clearly at the age of seventeen, and responded so positively, there she was at twenty-one, four years later, teaching home science.

'Ah, well I had to prove to God that I couldn't live as a religious, as a celibate.' She laughs, then, saying she's not quite sure how much to say. 'I mean I didn't live a very wild life but I did have several relationships. It was, you know, just a normal life.'

Yet life was difficult and while she was teaching she had to work at 'keeping body and soul together emotionally. There was a lot of healing that still needed to happen at that stage.'

When the call to the priesthood came she decided not to duck the issue of the religious life any longer but to 'to give it a go'. Joining the Community of the Sisters of the Church, which she did in 1972, was very much a trial, testing God to find out if she could live this way of life. As it turned out it was an eight-year trial because she didn't feel ready to make her final vows of poverty, chastity and obedience until 1981.

God of the impossible

'I believe in celibacy and I believe it's right for me but, you know, celibacy is a much bigger issue than just not having sex. It's a much more positive thing. I see celibacy as having to do with how well I love other people, and how I love myself and how I love God. I see the three tied in together. In today's society I feel it is a great challenge to live in appropriate loving relationships as a celibate, giving dignity to others.'

The years between 1982 and 1984 were spent at the community's house at Ham in Surrey, and were a very important period for her. During her training period she had been asked to lead quiet days like the one where I met her on Ash Wednesday 1998, and to talk to people about their relationship with God. She was, however, very aware that she hadn't been trained for that kind of work so from 1982–84 she trained in the giving of quiet days and in spiritual direction. She also studied Jungian psychology, which involved undertaking a course of Jungian therapy.

'Since then I have had a lot of short-term periods of therapy of various kinds, always choosing to work on a specific issue. I would describe my experience of therapy as "very blessed". The work I have done with therapists has been so creative; it has enabled me to connect with myself and the God of transformation, a God who is a God of healing and of love and who can change the past.'

The part of her past in most need of transformation, she says, was her childhood and adolescence. When speaking of that early part of her life, she uses words like 'brokenness' and 'pain' and 'chaos' but does not wish to speak in any detail about those times.

'What I had experienced needed to have something done with it by God. Which is really why I said what I said that Ash Wednesday when we met, about an awareness of sin being an awareness of God. That came from my early life:

the brokenness and the pain is what actually takes us into the God experience. God is within everything. God can do something with everything.'

The healing began with the therapy, she says. 'The work I did with the pain of my own life in therapy was very much a part of my spiritual journey. God was always present in that work, and I was always aware that God provided the right person at the right time. Again I would see God opening doors, providing.'

She stops and grins, and her tone changes to one of self mockery. 'I have a very strong sense of God providing but I sometimes get very impatient because the help is not being provided at the time when *I* want it, when *I* think I want it, or how I want it. Or put it another way: I often do not appreciate God's sense of humour. Oh, I have a wonderful awareness of it but I don't always appreciate it. So often the situations that I most resent or want to avoid and the people I find most uncomfortable, are the way that God reveals the path to love and healing!'

As important as therapy, says Linda Mary, is all the work she has done with community chaplains and with spiritual directors. For instance, with one chaplain she went over a particular year of her life at each of their monthly sessions, working backwards from the early 1980s. 'And it wasn't as if he gave me absolution so much as took the experiences of the whole year into God and then anointed me with holy oil. Some of the things were confession of sin but most were awareness of brokenness and painful experiences. That was very helpful to me. I had a very broad sense of God's healing light within my life.'

In Lent 1995 a trip to Israel to attend a three-week course at St George's College just outside the walls of Jerusalem proved deeply significant. The experience of walking where Jesus had walked – Mount Sinai, the Dead Sea,

Nazareth and Bethlehem – she found profoundly moving. 'I learned from my interaction with the place itself and also from the interaction with the other people on the course. I came home knowing I had to make a choice to be different. The whole experience of that time in Israel was pushing me to be more human. Everything was saying: "Linda, will you honour your humanity and your relationship with other people?"

'One day we went to the Mount of Transfiguration. We had about three or four hours there by ourselves. And I just sat on the top of that hill and I poured my heart out to God. What came out of that very clearly for me from God was "I *am* the God of the impossible. I am the God of transfiguration. Linda, let me do it." Over and over again through my life I hear God saying that, "Linda, let me do it."

'And I keep saying to Him, "Well, you know, God, it can't be that easy." There's part of me, perhaps part of all of us, that doesn't want to let go and lose control. It's as if part of me is holding back, saying: "Well, I can't quite see how you're going to do this."' She laughs at herself. 'That is just so absolutely me. I am constantly being challenged to stop trying to organise God – which I do often try to do – and to just let God be God.' Two years after she was in Israel she went to St Beuno's in North Wales to do the three-month course in apostolic spirituality which included training in giving the spiritual exercises of St Ignatius. 'I knew when I went there that I needed to be shown the human face of God. I needed to see in the face of a human being, something of the unconditional love of God. I needed to find a person who could show me a human face of God. You see, God's not a person. I mean God is whatever God is, but I knew that in my spiritual journey, because of a lot of my past experiences, I needed to experience the unconditional love that is God's gift to us, through another human being,

63

or as near as possible. And that happened at St Beuno's. And again it was God providing, and it was a great gift.

'St Beuno's also confirmed for me that my preference in ministry is spiritual direction and retreat work, journeying with people in their spiritual journey ... So, that's St Beuno's. It's linked, you know, with what happened in Israel: St Beuno's had to happen after Israel.'

Towards the end of our conversation Linda Mary says there is one aspect of her life that she hasn't yet talked about: her relationship with the land, with the land of Australia. When she was once again at the sisters' house in Ham in the late 1990s, she became convinced that when she went back home to Australia she had to go to the centre of Australia: to Uluru (Ayers Rock), and to Alice Springs. 'I had not given myself the opportunity to experience God in the centre of my own country, Australia.

'And for me, driving out into the centre of the country, being in the centre, experiencing the centre, has turned out to be a returning to *my* centre, a centre I probably never knew I had. Now if I just go back to my childhood ... I didn't have a space that I could call my own, or call home, or a place that was safe. So as a child I didn't grow up feeling that wonderful sense of security one would hope all children have.

'Going to the centre has given me that. It is a place where I have found myself crossing many thresholds, but it is also a place where I have found something of my truth and, in inverted commas, a "security". There has also been a sense of coming home to the land. I would never have said that as a child I was connected to the land but I must have been because I can now connect with it again. It feels like a re-connection – but it feels like a place that is truer.

'The rock, Uluru, is this enormous rock and about 90 per cent of it is submerged; we only see the top part of it. And for me life is like that, people only see that little top part but there's a whole world underneath. And you see, what's happening for me in this experience of living simply in the centre, sleeping in a tent, going to bed when the sun goes down and getting up when it rises, is that it's getting me in contact with the underneath, the other side. And I have a great respect for the centre, for the aridness of our land; all of that is fruitful for me. So the centre for me is terribly important: I keep going back to listen more deeply and to feel more the life of the land and my own centre and God within and each time there is a sense of the next step; a deeper connecting to come.'

She is quiet for a few seconds then.

'It's like ... when I was a child there was a sense of something pushing me. And I hung on, looking for something more. Which is what I am still doing now. Not in the sense of hanging on but I'm still pushing the boundaries, you know, looking for the more of God, the bigger of God, the God that can transform absolutely everything.

'For me transfiguration, the changing of something into something else, is vital. It is vital that God is the God of transfiguration. God really is for me the God of transfiguration, the God of the impossible.'

Chapter 8

'There is no objective God'

I had been looking forward to the meeting for learning that was about to begin, following the meeting for worship, for some time. Graham, our clerk at Richmond Quaker Meeting, who had spoken at the first conference of the Sea of Faith group some years earlier, was going to talk to us about their group.

I had been confused about the group's beliefs ever since I'd seen a series of television programmes in the 1980s entitled *The Sea of Faith*, which had been written and presented by Don Cupitt, an Anglican priest and Cambridge academic and theologian. The series had aimed, it seemed to me, at updating religious thinking and ideas about God, drawing perhaps most of all on the work of Kierkegaard. I found the programmes very interesting but was shocked when the conclusion seemed to be that the practice of religion was for its own sake, because it made us better people. It seemed God was not part of the picture.

There was something of a furore at the time and Cupitt was accused of being an atheist. When his book, which had the same title as the TV series, came out, I bought it and read it, seeking clarification. It took the same line as the programmes. I was very confused because he continued as an Anglican priest, took services, and prayed yet seemed to be saying that there was no God to pray to.

So I was hoping that Graham would clear up some of my concerns and perhaps reassure me that the Sea of Faith group could not be Christians and atheists at the same time.

What he said, however, amongst other things, was: 'There is no objective God. God is a human construct.' Now of course I know that God is not a thing, an object, an old man with a white beard in the sky, and that all talk of him – even 'him' – is metaphorical. I believe God is mystery and unknowable in any ordinary everyday sense of the word. But I don't believe that he is 'not'.

Graham also said that the God he was talking about was not one you could pray to for nice weather for your holidays or a win on the lottery, which I accepted completely. But two big questions began to plague me: what can you pray to God for and about if he is simply a human construct? And how different is it to say that God is a human construct than to say God is a figment of our imagination?

Another thing Graham said seemed to contradict what he had said earlier, namely that 'when Christ became incarnate, the distance between God and us disappeared ...' Far from being reassured I was more confused and distressed than ever. Over the next couple of days I found myself crying on and off. It was like being in an emotional earthquake: I could no longer rely on the ground beneath my feet. In an attempt to find some sort of equilibrium I kept reminding myself that Christ said that when we pray we should say 'Our Father' and that when the storm first blew up about the Sea of Faith group, I'd read a quote from a bishop in a newspaper, which said that God was 'never less than personal'. But I still felt lost and shaken.

In the Spring of the year 2000, I had written to Sister Linda Mary, who had been back in Australia for some time, asking if she would be my spiritual director by correspondence. She had agreed. Now I remembered something she said during one of our sessions at the 1998 retreat. She'd said that Christ was angrier about what had been done to me than I was. That had continued to astonish me: it made Christ so real. Everything I was feeling now was pushing me somehow in the opposite direction. I was in the quicksand of doubt and could find nothing to hang onto. But at least I could write to her about all this. I found that even just writing the letter helped a bit. As did talking to Avril, the psychotherapist who was helping me with my long-standing and worsening problem of fear of flying. She asked if I felt as if my 'faith had been challenged'. That put it into words for me. It was not an easy session and I was still troubled when I came away, though a random and little-regarded phrase popped into my head (*the first time I wrote about this instead of 'head' I wrote 'home'*) a couple of times: 'Good will come of this.'

I remained, however, in turmoil and kept getting into knots as I tried to untangle the problem. Then I remembered something that Avril had said at the psychotherapy session, namely that I 'give a lot of power' to people who I think have achieved 'success'. Graham is an ex-Oxford don and a theologian, which puts him high up in my 'awesome success' category. Could that be part of it?

I was still stuck and still miserable when, on the Friday morning following the meeting for learning of the previous Sunday, a letter arrived. It was from a stranger in response to a letter of mine which had been published in *The Friend*, the weekly magazine and newsletter of the Quakers. In it I had complained fairly mildly and in a jokey way about the bureaucracy of Quaker organisation.

But the person who had written to me did not mention Quaker organisation: he was looking for a Quaker pen-friend. He was a patient in a Special Hospital, a secure mental hospital for people with mental, emotional or psychological problems who have committed crimes and who are thought to be dangerous to themselves or others. I'd visited the hospital to interview woman patients for my book, *Doubly Deviant: Doubly Damned,* which is about how the criminal justice system treats women who have committed violent crimes. I had found it to be a truly dreadful place, frightening, and full of frightened people.

Michael said he was a Christian with rather unorthodox views. He'd been reading *The Friend* for some years and had decided to seek a penfriend 'to help me in my spiritual life'. His spiritual life centred on Jesus although he was 'rather agnostic' about God so he focused more on Jesus the man 'who teaches me how I should live and what I should do'.

With this letter the turmoil ceased. Michael had replied to my concerns of the previous week. A prayer that hadn't been articulated, that in the circumstances could hardly be prayed, had been answered. Here was another seeker who, while uncertain and 'rather agnostic' about God, was nevertheless trying to keep going, and against far greater odds than me. I was now no longer in an agony of mind but I still had a residual problem: where did I go from here? It didn't feel finished.

In the middle of the next night, Saturday, I woke up, was suddenly wide awake, and knew what I had to do. I had to speak about all this, to 'minister', as Quakers put it, at meeting for worship in the morning. Help! I couldn't do that. It was too much. And suppose Graham was offended. How could I speak about this? I just couldn't do it. The resistance didn't last long, however, because I had learned through previous experience how strong the feeling of the need to minister is. I went back to sleep.

When I ministered about what had happened that Sunday morning I said Graham had spoken about the Sea of Faith at our request, both eloquently and with great sincerity, and that I thanked him for it, but that I had left the meeting troubled in my mind and in some distress. I talked about the problem having been put into words and then I spoke about Michael's letter. I read out the part of it that was to do with spirituality.

I added that more than one or two friends present would know how much I valued a book by Gerard Hughes, *God of Surprises*, and that, well, this had indeed been a very surprising week. Which was when, just as I was about to sit down, there came another surprise: my throat tightened, my voice broke and I began to cry. Later in the meeting Graham ministered on the meaning of 'grace'.

One thing I didn't mention was that that morning before coming to meeting I had reached page 60 of a re-reading of yet another book by Gerard Hughes, *God, Where Are You?*, having completely forgotten what was coming next. He is writing about studying philosophy. I can't do better than quote it here.

> The subject I found most obscure was ontology, the study of being. It was all so abstract, and the various theses on the analogy of being contained most complex terminology. It was only years later that I began to understand the importance and relevance of this subject. As I write the press and media are full of reports and commentary on an Anglican vicar who has been expelled from his parish by his bishop because he says he no longer believes in God. [As far as I recall this priest was a member of the Sea of Faith group.] In the ensuing controversy I have heard nothing on St Thomas's teaching on the analogy of being. I am a being, you are a being, and God is a being, but God's beingness is not the same as yours and mine. The word 'being' can only be used

analogously of God, because God is always beyond, always greater than anything our minds can conceive or imagine. In our human sense of being, it would be true to say that God is not a being, as we experience being, and it is therefore true to say that in our sense of exist, God does not exist.

When people say, 'I no longer believe in God', their assertion must be respected, but they must be encouraged to examine what it is they no longer believe. To question the notion of God which we have been taught is a necessary stage in the faith journey. If someone says, 'I no longer believe in God', meaning that they can no longer accept the notion of God as a separate, all-powerful super-being external to us, who controls all things, but whose beingness is the same as ours, only greater, then that person may, in fact, be moving to a deeper understanding of God ... I now no longer feel disturbed if someone says, 'I no longer believe in God'. I feel much more disturbed when I meet someone who has never entertained a doubt and claims to have an unshakeable faith in God.[1]

Before Linda had time to reply to my letter I was able to write and tell her about the resolution/resurrection/victory. She quickly got back to me to say that perhaps the essence of the experience was that 'God is within everything, even when it feels as it did for you – terrible turmoil – and like Jesus in Holy Week, and on Good Friday, it was something that needed to be lived through, and only in the living through it, open to surprises, can the resolution/resurrection/victory come.'

[1] Gerard W. Hughes, *God, Where Are You?* (Darton, Longman and Todd, 1997), pp. 59–60.

Chapter 9

A candle in the church

The cream people-carrier I shared with five strangers stopped outside Ince Parish Church where the funeral service was to be held. I got out and stood alone on the pavement, my arms clasped tight in front of me to keep warm as the wind stung my eyes and pinched at the lobes of my ears beneath my black beret. I pulled the belt of my black coat tight, trying to keep in any heat. The others stood around talking to each other in low voices, their eyes flicking away from the sight of the hearse and the coffin.

My mother had gone to Ince Parish. In 1931, aged twenty, she'd been given a Bible as a prize for good attendance at Sunday School. What had the vicar's name been then? I could remember my Mum talking about him, and rolling her eyes at the very thought of anybody daring to disagree with him. Had it been Stoneley? Yes, that was it, Reverend Stoneley. Seven years after getting that prize at Sunday School, she'd married my Dad in a Roman Catholic church and stopped attending her own church in deference to him until after her own fiercely Protestant mother had died, when she'd felt free to convert to Catholicism. She told me at the time, that she was converting simply because she wanted to go to church again. 'What's it matter which church you go to? There's only one God.' So, to please my Dad she'd given up going to Ince Parish, and so as not to offend her mother she had refused to become a Catholic. Of course, in order for the marriage to take place in a Roman Catholic church, she'd had to promise that any children of the marriage would be brought up Roman Catholic. I was the only one.

It was, in a roundabout way, because of Mum, who'd now been dead for six years, that I was standing outside the parish church on this bitter January morning. I was here to attend the funeral of Roy, the husband of a close friend of mine, Cynthia, who'd first of all been a close friend of Mum's.

Cynthia had been the secretary of 'the big boss', as Mum described him, at the paintworks where Mum had worked as the tea lady. That had been twenty-five years ago and now I was close friends not only with Cynthia but with her elder daughter, Wendy, as well, continuing the pattern of inter-generational friendships started by Mum and Cynthia. Mum had been in her sixties when she'd made friends with Cynthia who had then been in her late thirties. Now Cynthia was just sixty, I was fifty-six, and Wendy thirty-eight.

I was here to be of what support I could and out of fondness and respect for Roy, a gentle, quiet man who liked his rollups, and a pint or two – at home, he didn't go to the pub – and who had been an obsessive builder of things. As long as I'd known him he'd had a cough and hadn't been able to work because of his chest. And somehow, because he'd always been 'not quite well', I suppose we'd all taken it for granted that he'd go on still being 'not quite well' into old age. But he'd died suddenly on New Year's Day, while Cynthia was in India visiting relatives.

Cynthia's relatives in India were not expats; despite her so English-sounding name, Cynthia was part Chinese and part Malaysian and had only come to Lancashire at the age of fifteen. She spoke, however, just like the rest of us, with a Lancashire accent. But she also spoke Mandarin.

I reflected that as this was her parish church, and she'd always been a regular churchgoer, she'd know the vicar, which was something: at least the vicar would know one member of the family. Not that he would have known Roy, who never went near the church. I felt my jaw tightening as I contemplated listening to some unctuous cleric intone piously about Roy, whom he'd never met. How could he possibly know that Roy was as good a man as any who regularly showed up at services, if not better.

I pulled myself up, telling myself to just get through the funeral, that it would soon be over, and that then I'd be around for Cynthia and Wendy. As I let my gaze wander along the bleak row of terraced houses facing the church, out of the corner of my eye I caught the swirl of a black cloak and a flash of bright purple. The vicar had arrived. I turned to inspect him. Above the cloak bounced shiny black curls; thick black eyelashes fringed clear grey eyes above a wide mouth. Oh. The vicar was a woman. A young, vivacious and pretty woman. Now she was speaking to the elderly couple in front me as we went into the church. Oh. The vicar was a scouser, a Liverpudlian. And her earrings were small crystal crosses.

Ouch. What an uncomfortable sensation. I was being forced to look at my own prejudices, something I thought only other people had. Confronted by this gently smiling young woman, I felt as if deep inside tectonic plates of what had been immovable beliefs were shifting: and I didn't like it. I had been anti-vicars and anti-'the Church' for so long (with certain, very few exceptions which, I told myself, only proved the rule) that the beliefs felt as much part of me as my bones. My credo on churches was: churches and vicars were past it, they just didn't know it yet. The rest of us had moved on and most people didn't think about the Church from one decade to the next. Oh, sure it was useful for a full-blown wedding, provided a nice setting – more atmosphere than the Register Office, more romantic – and it was useful for those few people who still liked a christening, but even then it was more of a social marker than an expression of faith. And of course, it was psychologically useful for funerals. But as for being a part of real life, getting its hands dirty, being in the thick of people's problems, joys, struggles and sorrows, forget it. Definitely sidelined by the start of the twenty-first century, the institution of the Church was a leftover from previous centuries, in imminent danger of extinction because it was too stiff, too old and too rigid to change. Well past its sell-by date.

But this young woman was most definitely not past it. So, I said to myself, watching her closely as she turned to face the congregation, let's see what kind of a job she'll make of the funeral of a non-churchgoer she's never met.

She began by speaking of Jesus weeping at the graveside of his friend, Lazarus. 'But his tears weren't a sign of weakness, but of his great compassion for the family and friends left behind.'

She assured us that 'God grieves with you in your loss, because Roy, and indeed all of us here, are important to Him.'

She didn't intone, and she didn't adopt a pious pose. Her voice was just the same as when she'd greeted us at the entrance to the church, completely lacking in affectation. And she so clearly believed every word she was saying that she had no need to try and impress us with the depth of her belief. It was just there, as real as breathing. She admitted that while she knew Cynthia well, she hadn't met Roy, but, having spoken to Cynthia, she had found out a little bit about Roy's life. 'A typical Lancashire lad' was how Cynthia had described him, she said, and then began to talk about Roy's falconry, his love of walking in the countryside until ill health kept him at home, and his passion for model building. 'He was always borrowing, persuading and cadging to get the materials he needed to make a steam train, an aeroplane or a yacht.'

I visualised the full-size boat in the backyard which Roy had been working on for years, looking forward to the whole family having a canal holiday on it. But now she was talking about how Roy could be really 'laid back in his outlook, which Cynthia said did annoy her sometimes'. She gave a wide grin as she spoke and I smiled to myself as I remembered Cynthia – one of the most 'let's get going and get it done' people I have ever met – chafing with irritation at Roy's slow and leisurely pace of life.

The young woman went on to talk about how Roy 'loved his music. But not content with just listening, he repaired mandolins and fiddles to their former glory, and, after a pint or two or three, loved a good old singsong.'

She then said we would have a moment or two of silence so that each of us could remember Roy and what he meant to us. I remembered the gentleness in his eyes, and the wonderful curries he made. And when she began to speak again, I found that once more, I was smiling.

'In the introductory sentences, I read some words from St John's Gospel: "Jesus said, I am the resurrection and I am the life. He who believes in me, though he die, yet shall he live. And whoever lives and believes in me shall never die."

'The passage of Scripture goes on to ask the question: "Do you believe this?" And that question equally applies to you and to me now. For when the love of God is present in our hearts, we, like Jesus, conquer the power of death.

'In the temptation to lose faith, we will trust the one who loved us to the end.

'In the temptation to give way to despair, we will hope in the one who rose from the grave.

'In the love of Christ – during this life – we will not find the answers to all our questions. But, I believe that God can carry us – as on a wave – through all our doubts and fears, till one day with Christ in glory all our questions will be answered. Amen.'

For a few seconds we remained sitting in silence. But this was a quite different silence from that at the start of the service. Something had happened. Somehow this young woman had banished the morbidness, the mawkishness, and the superstitious dread of death. The grief and the loss were still there, there had been no denying of them. But now the grief would not turn septic; it wasn't going to fester, to turn inwards to poison the system. The grief, the loss and the fear of death, in some strange way, had been embraced. A metamorphosis had occurred.

When I turn up for our interview at her terraced house just across the road from the parish church, she's out. But a very few minutes later she comes running down the street, hair and cloak flying. As she lets us in she explains she was taking a funeral. There's a flurry of smiles and apologies as she pulls off dog collar, white surplice, and long black gown to reveal trim black trousers and a black cardigan with a spray of deep pink and red roses picked out by the neck. She smiles, thinking about the funeral she has just conducted, saying 'It was special, really. Special.' Then she shrugs off her introspection, laughing, and tells us about the old men at the funeral patting her on the head and asking: 'Will you do mine, love, when it's my turn?'

'They're always doing that,' she says to me, clucking her tongue against her teeth in mock disapproval but smiling to show she doesn't mind at all really, but only finds it funny that they think of her as a little girl.

As she goes into the kitchen to see to the tea I stand by the window, looking out at the terraced houses opposite, as the cold January light fades above the slate roofs. They are so familiar to me, these streets; I was born and brought up here. There must have been a time, when I was a child, when I didn't hate them. But I can't remember it. Just two streets away from here is one that still has cobbles. Bird Street. My mother, who worked in 't'factory' for more than twenty years, was born in Bird Street. I turn from the window and my gaze falls on a big black-and-white photograph hanging above the sofa. It's of women workers sitting on a piece of scaffolding sticking out into thin air from the top of a Manhattan skyscraper. I am still wondering about this photograph when Linda comes in with the tea and we sit down to talk.

She begins her story in South East Romania, where, she says, her life changed direction. 'That's where everything got turned on its head.' And the person responsible for the change was a priest of the Eastern Orthodox Church (of which she knew nothing) who spoke barely a word of English.

She went to Romania as a photographer. The job was straightforward: a commission from some friends, who were architects, to take pictures of a community school which they were helping to build, and of the people who would benefit from the school. The photographs would be used in an exhibition to raise funds for the project. But at present there was only enough money in the kitty to cover her flight and the cost of her film.

At the time she and her boyfriend, Jimmy, also a photographer, lived in a nice flat in a fashionable part of London and her career had really taken off. Her work was being published in newspapers such as the *Independent* and the *Sunday Times*, and in various glossy magazines. The BBC rang her for help with research, wanting contacts. She had more work than she could handle. Life was really buzzing.

'But, you know, inside, inside me there was something missing. And for a long time I'd not stopped working. What I'd said at the start was I'll do all these jobs and then every so often I'll take a couple of weeks off and just do my own documentary work, you know, take the photographs *I* want to take. That had been the great idea. But it never happened. So when this came up I thought "What the hell, go for it, it'll be a break. What is it – two weeks of your life? Go for it, help them out."'

So she went. And she stayed not for two weeks but for a year.

It didn't take her long to get enough shots of everything she needed. But then she realised that there was one place where she hadn't taken any photographs: the church. And she'd noticed that everybody went to church. So off she went to the church and, using sign language, and such French as she could remember from school – the only language they had in common – she asked the local priest, Father Costika, known as Father Tiki, if she could take pictures inside the church. He said yes, she could, after the service had ended.

'So I just sat there, through the service, and all the people kept looking at me. And I wondered why they were all looking at me; then I thought, "Oh, it's the cameras, it's because of the cameras." But I found out afterwards that it wasn't the cameras. I'd been sitting on the men's side of the church, instead of the women's! I didn't even know they had men's and women's sides in the church. But everybody laughed about it when they told me and they were all really lovely with me.'

Father Tiki began showing her around the town, introducing her to people, and taking her into their homes with him. She found that the two of them got on well together and that they were able to communicate 'as people', despite the problems with language.

'He'd touch me on the shoulder and then touch his eyes and point. And there'd be an old lady, sitting in her home. And I'd think, what is he trying to make me see, I've taken the picture, what more does he want? And the old lady would talk and he'd make me sit down and listen, even though I couldn't understand. He let me see people's lives, and where they were, and what a privilege it was to be allowed into somebody's home ... They had a faith, these people. And he'd pray with them. He was a real priest, a real priest in every sense of the word. He loved his people and they loved him; you could see it and feel it. I used to try and photograph him in these special moments. That was always a thrill for me, trying to capture that moment and I really tried but I failed because it was something that was felt. And it didn't come out on a camera. And I sat and observed him and I just saw love, and God again in a way that I'd never known.'

By this time she'd been away longer than the planned two weeks and her friends back in London were wondering what she was doing, speculating that she must be researching something 'really heavy'. She changed her return flight to a later date, hardly conscious of how the weeks were passing, and continued going with Father Tiki to the homes of people in the town, to the local orphanage, and to meet the gypsies in the area, to learn a little about their way of life. What she was doing was documenting Father Tiki's life but she ended up putting her camera down. 'I thought: "It's OK, I can put my camera down. It's OK, I don't have to hide behind this camera. Even though

I've only been here a few weeks I'm accepted. I've become part of the town."

'I remember sitting in church one day; Father Tiki was celebrating. I was just sitting, looking at the crucifix, when I remembered what I'd been taught as a child about the crucifix. I guess the thing that stuck in my mind about this was SIN. The emphasis on this had been overwhelming. Jesus was only on this cross because I was a bad girl – I'd been born 'bad'. Whenever I entered the church (or even walked passed it on my way to school), I would either hang my head in shame or frown rebelliously at it – but both actions carried feelings of guilt. The feeling of wanting to scream loudly and say my sincere, deep heartfelt 'sorry' to God was, at times, quite overwhelming. I remained trapped in these feelings of guilt until adult life.

'It's funny; I didn't really remember as much emphasis being put on the Resurrection – and there was certainly no mention of the *joy* of Jesus having defeated death. And words like love and grace, which I'm sure must have been mentioned (or perhaps they weren't), got lost somewhere along the line.

'That day in Romania when I sat looking at the crucifix I felt showered with feelings of overwhelming love. God became personal – so much so that the guilt that I had carried seemed to fall away. I felt God give me a great big bear hug – I know this probably sounds really naff but I did feel it – soothing my innermost hurts and pains. I could do nothing but let the tears fall. Tears of relief that God was my friend and tears of joy because for once in my life I knew that I belonged – like the Prodigal Son the father had come out to greet me with open arms.'

Linda decided to stay on in Romania. But while at one level she felt 'all right' about her decision, at another level she was afraid. For one thing, she knew she would lose all her contacts in London. 'I knew life was never going to be the same again and I was frightened because I'd worked so hard to achieve what I had in London but I knew I wasn't ever going back there. What I didn't know was what I *was* going to do. It was, you know, like: "What *am* I going to do? Help!"'

Once she had made the decision to stay on for a year she phoned Jimmy, in London, to tell him. He flew out to see her. 'The only word I think he heard was "staying" and he thought: "What have I done? What's happening?" Before I went to Romania we'd been chasing a big job in China: we were going to do it together, as a couple. This was the big one. And we'd got it. And now I was telling him he'd have to go on his own. But I couldn't tell him why. I could only say I couldn't really put my finger on it, but that, well, I supposed I'd become a Christian.

'He was always very supportive of me and tried to understand but he wanted me to come home. He said that, OK, I had a belief, but that this was our life: was I going to let God come before us? Didn't I think I was taking this God thing too seriously?

'I didn't even say anything; it was too late. It had already happened. I remember Jimmy just sitting there and he looked around and he said: "You left Norris Green, which was a dump, and now your whole life is changing and you're sitting in a dump again and you're saying you want to stay."

'And he was right, I had, I'd come full circle but this time I'd chosen it, it was a conscious decision. Even though I had no idea what the future would hold, it just felt so right. I just had to go with it.'

Norris Green, where Linda was born in 1967, is a huge council estate on the outskirts of Liverpool. The houses, which were built just after the Second World War, were meant to be temporary but are still there today.

Her Dad is, she says, with a smile 'a traditional Liverpudlian male'. He worked on the docks, was a shop steward, was the Man of the House and liked a pint. But he was also 'a real armchair traveller' and used to take Linda, her elder sister Barbara and her brother Michael down to the docks and point out all the different flags on the ships and tell them about all the different countries they came from.

'An evening's entertainment at home would be watching travel documentaries on telly, which was very unusual for that estate', says Linda with a grin and a raised eyebrow to indicate just how unusual it was. Her Mum didn't share this fascination with foreign and faraway places; in fact she was so completely content with her home in Norris Green that she never even wanted to go on holiday.

It was Linda's sister Barbara who saw the importance of education for Linda. 'She was five years older than me, we shared a bedroom, and when she came home from school she'd get her schoolbooks out and play school teacher with me. By the time I started school I was quite advanced.'

The family, 'the Rileys' (they called themselves 'the clan'), were one of the really big Liverpool Irish Catholic families. Her Mum, however, was from an 'Orange' family; she was Church of England. When her Mum and Dad got married – in the Catholic Church – there was a huge fight between the two families, and the police had to be called in to sort it out. She can remember family members making snide remarks about her Mum on Orange Day, saying things like "Oh, yer takin' the kids on the march then, are yer?" But Mum never got involved in religious politics.'

It was only when she was seven, the age that Roman Catholic children make their first Holy Communion, that Linda discovered she wasn't a Roman Catholic. Until then she had always thought she was a Catholic. She went to

Catholic school, she went to Mass, she *was* a Catholic.

'Then when we were all preparing for Holy Communion Father Pat said: "You can't, Linda." I said: "What do you mean, I can't? I come to church all the time." And he told me I'd been baptised Church of England. And I never knew. No one ever told me. And I remember thinking, "I'm not going to be able to wear the white dress." I felt a real outsider. And I mean the whole class, all my special friends in the street, they were all going to get dressed up. And I couldn't. But it was more than just the dress and the veil, the dressing up. I loved going to church. I had a sense even then of knowing God in the way a seven-year-old can. I liked going to Confession, and I liked Father Pat. But now, I could go to church and to Confession but I couldn't go to Communion. So I still carried on going to church but I always felt like I'd been cheated of the party cake. And kids can be awful. At Mass when it was time to go up to the altar rails for Holy Communion they'd say: "You've got to sit there. You can't come." And I'd sit there thinking, "Why's this happening to me?"

'I remember asking Mum if I could become a Catholic and she said I could decide when I was older. She said, "You're all right as yer are." I had the feeling of knowing my faith inside, knowing God inside but never really belonging. In some important way I was excluded: I was part of something but I didn't truly belong. I think from then on I always felt sort of different.'

Nor did she fit in at the comprehensive school she went to at the age of eleven. Being a bright little girl, she had the chance to go to a grammar school on the other side of Liverpool. She'd cried and cried to be allowed to go; she remembers her sister Barbara screaming at their parents that she must be allowed to go. She remembers the headmaster from her primary school coming to the door and

pleading with her Mum and Dad not to throw away this
'wonderful opportunity for Linda'. But the school was a
bus ride away and a young girl had been raped near it and
her Mum said Barbara had done well at the local comprehensive and Michael was all right there too so she could
go there as well. And anyway, her Mum said, if she went to
the local comprehensive, she could come home for her
dinner if she wanted.

'So I went to this awful school. And I hated it from the
day I started until the day I left.' But, much as she loathed
the school, it was there she met Robin Lloyd, an English
teacher, who introduced her to photography. 'Whenever I
think of the word "grace" I think of him.

'The school was a typical run down comprehensive
school and if there's one thing that *was* taught there, sadly,
it was that pupils shouldn't set their sights too high. We
lived in a run down area, went to a run down school – if we
were lucky enough to be offered any job, then regardless of
what it was we should take it. As the saying goes, "beggars
can't be choosers".

'To have this drummed into you day in and day out
knocks out all hopes and dreams. But Robin wasn't your
normal run-of-the-mill teacher – he was passionate about
his teaching. He encouraged pupils. He saw their potential.
He allowed us to dream our dreams, so to speak. When I
picked up his camera – having been told not to – and then
carelessly dropped it, Robin could have had me in de-
tention for a month. But he showed me true grace: he
forgave me when I didn't deserve to be forgiven. He could
see I was truly sorry. And rather than sending me away he
turned this awful embarrassing situation into something
positive – teaching me how to hold a camera properly, and
showing me how to develop the film. Little did he know
that this generous act of forgiveness would be the start of

something incredible for me, life-changing in fact. A chain of events followed on from a broken camera: a love of photography; a gift nurtured and developed; access to travel the world; to Romania; to God.

'My camera has been a key with which I have opened many doors in my life. I have met so many wonderful people and have seen and done things that wouldn't have been possible if I had remained in Norris Green. Eventually God used this skill of mine to open the door of my heart.

'Robin also inspired me to see beauty all around me. What, I thought? In Norris Green? That stopped me in my tracks. "Record your life, your estate, the people," he said. And I did. I couldn't stop taking pictures.'

She was sixteen when she sold her first photograph. It was of her Dad at his workplace: he'd worked for a ship-building firm that had started two hundred years ago and now it was closing down. When the *Liverpool Echo* published her photograph and paid her for it she couldn't believe it. 'I thought, "Hey, they pay you for this. That's even better."'

Robin Lloyd encouraged her to try for a place studying photography at a college in Newport, South Wales. She didn't know at the time but the competition for places was fierce. She was accepted but had to find £5,000 in fees.

'So I left Liverpool and went to live with an uncle in Bournemouth and I had a set plan. I'd take any job going and just work and work and work and save until I had the money.' By dint of working all the time – including a stint in a bath mat factory – she got the money. And then went back to Liverpool and worked as a community arts photographer until the next academic year began.

By this time, in her late teens, she'd drifted away from church. 'I never really got over not being allowed to make my first Holy Communion; it seemed like I'd never fit in, like they were never going to let me fit in.' She'd gone through a phase around the age of fourteen to sixteen when sometimes she helped with the children at an independent inner city mission where she went to services occasionally. 'But I never really felt I belonged there either. I suppose I just got bored. There was nothing. I got fed up, I was not quite an adult but not a child. And I stopped going. I didn't stop believing in God. I just felt God wasn't relevant in my life, if I thought about God at all … But it doesn't leave you, does it?'

Her work as a community arts photographer was centred on the disabled. She used her camera to highlight disability issues and found she had 'a real love and a passion for community'. She realised that photographs could help get things changed, make life better for people: it wasn't just about taking pictures.

In college in Newport she found her niche. She fitted right in. Here she was understood. She loved everything about it, felt 'completely at home'. She learned a lot on the course, and not only about photography. For one exercise they each had to pick a topic from a hat and then go and do a series of photographs about it. Linda picked out poaching. 'I thought, "Help! I'm a city girl, what do I know about poaching?"' So she did what seemed to her the only thing to do: she got a train up the Wye valley into the country, went into the local pub and asked the landlord if he knew anything about poaching. He said he didn't, but that one or two of the men in the corner over there might. She talked to the men and to their girlfriends. They got on. One man had been in jail in Liverpool and had fond memories of the place and the people! She got spectacular shots of poaching – including one of a bath full of salmon. The pictures ended up in the *Sunday Times*. And she had learned something about herself that she hadn't known before: people trusted her, and pretty quickly too.

Of the people she met on the course she singles out one of the lecturers, Daniel Meadows, as having a special influence. He led a discussion one day about whether you take the picture first and think about the ethics second. Do you just take the picture and let the editor worry about the ethics?

'He was very clear that you think first about what you are doing and why. Only when you've answered those questions do you shoot the picture. Or maybe you don't. He told us not to forget we were human beings when we took photographs and so were the people we were photographing. He said "Be in control of your own work, you're the one who has to lie in bed later and think what you've done."'

Linda remembers one part of the discussion in particular. 'Suppose you're in a situation where a guard comes to get you; they are going to shoot someone, execute him. Do you go along and take the picture or not? Perhaps if you take the picture it might help stop things like that happening again. But I said, "What if it didn't, what if you'd showed no compassion, if you didn't take a stand and say that no, you were refusing to take that photograph?" The others thought you should take the picture. Then I said: "I don't think God would want you to take the picture." And they all burst out laughing, saying "Who?" But I said: "We're talking about love and compassion here, so God's got to come into it." "Oh, my word," they all went, "the Irish Roman Catholic background really dominates you, doesn't it?" I was embarrassed. But it just came straight out. If I'd stopped to think about it it would have been hard to say but it just happened.'

When she came back from Romania the friends she'd

made in London through her work as a photographer kidded her. 'They'd say: "Lin went off with a camera and she came back with a Bible." And it was true.'

She smiles as she remembers but, she says, at the time she was frightened. She'd been fearful of leaving Romania. 'But it was time to leave. I knew, but I was scared. What was I going back to? I had nowhere to go. I had nothing to go back to. So where did I go back to? Norris Green.' She shakes her head at the memory of it. Photography, success, Romania, now she was going back to Norris Green – as what? She didn't know herself.

'Father Tiki was amazing those last few weeks in Romania. He was really strong for me. He encouraged me to come home. But what was I going to tell my Mum and Dad? How could I ever make them understand? And financially they'd supported me: each of them throughout my career had helped me financially and had supported me through many a tough patch. I will be forever grateful to them. They'd given me their all because I just had to be a photographer. And now it was all over. What was I going to say to them? Father Tiki said to serve the Church and serve God, that Christ would go ahead of me and I just had to follow. But I thought I can't say *that*, I can't go back and tell them that. I've got no plan.

'The family were all still there. My sister Barbara lived five minutes away from my Mum and Dad; she was working as a secretary. My brother Michael was as happy as Larry working as a painter and decorator. Nobody had moved. Static. It was amazing. It was like a Lowry painting: nobody moves. And I go back and fit right back into my little place – our Lin. But I was still different. I didn't fit in. It was like when I was doing photography and it was a really exciting time for me and I really wanted to share it with them. And they'd ask me what I was doing and they'd try and understand but within a minute or two of me trying to tell them all about it, what it was like, show them how exciting it was, they were bored. They'd be talking about other things. *Coronation Street*. Whatever. I knew they were really proud of me but I didn't want them only to be proud of me, I wanted to share it, I wanted them to understand me. I wanted them to know what I was feeling but I couldn't share it ... I suppose there has to be an acceptance somewhere but to be honest even now, at this point in my life, it's still there ... I used to joke sometimes and say perhaps I was parachuted in. It's been like that since I was seven...'

Her family's reaction to her homecoming was what she expected. 'At first their overall thought was that I would take up where I had left off – that I'd continue to be a professional photographer but this time basing myself in Liverpool. It was almost as if my time in Romania had just been some sort of gap year in my career. Even though they had never fully understood my photography they knew that I was good enough – lucky enough – to get paid for doing it. To help pay the bills, I even did a few commercial assignments within the first few weeks of my return, but we are a close family and it didn't take them long to notice that my heart wasn't in what I was doing. In many ways I'm sure they thought that I had lost the plot because I was throwing away a perfectly good career. To own a home, a car, have a credit card, holidays, is what most people on that estate dream of. I'd had it all and now here I was choosing with my own free will to give it all up.

'Norris Green is considered poor, with most people on the estate living below the poverty line, yet everything around me seemed to be caught in the materialistic trap that I had freed myself from in Romania. I knew God had a plan for me here but I was starting to lose sight of this, or maybe

I was starting to feel guilty for being different again, I'm still not too sure which.

'In order to pay my way at home I got a part-time night job in a local nursing home as an auxiliary nurse – besides feeling useful again in caring for the elderly mentally ill residents, it also meant my days were free to help in church and the community.'

When people asked her what had happened to the photography, she somehow found the courage to say what Father Tiki had suggested: 'I told them I still loved photography but I loved God more. To say that I loved God more than my photography was the truth – I guess in many ways it was such a personal and unexpected remark that most people were either gobsmacked or thought I was insane.'

Her first voluntary work came through a friend who told her they needed a volunteer to help with the playgroup at a local Anglican church. She threw herself into the work and soon branched out, seeing what needed to be done, and doing it. She got to know the people in the local community, becoming, in effect a community worker, as she had in Romania. 'I loved it, loved working with the people, loved the people.

'I realised that what the church in Romania had, and what the churches in Norris Green didn't have, was a real sense of community. People in Romania used the church buildings for community activities, and this brought people together. Norris Green was an area that, at that time, had few amenities that people could use – a few local shops and primary schools. Even if community groups had wanted to meet they would have had to go out of the area. So with the support of the church I promoted the church in the neighbourhood. At first the community was wary. "What's the catch?" they would ask. "If we use your hall, are you expecting to see us on Sunday in church?" The answer was that although they would be very welcome to come to church whenever, we wouldn't be looking down our noses at them if they didn't: the church was their parish church, it belonged to them, it existed in order to be used and not just for a couple of hours on a Sunday.

'A lot of my time was spent encouraging and supporting individuals to dream their dreams, and helping to initiate community activities. Line dancing; providing for the elderly; majorettes; art classes; computer courses; karate; cooking and sewing; youth clubs; health forums; small businesses; a parent and toddler group; men's groups; women's groups; a teenagers' base; a contact centre where separated parents can have supervised contact with their children; a drugs rehabilitation centre; keep-fit; Weight-Watchers; luncheon clubs, and an after school club – the church literally became the hub of the community. At one point there were over 1,000 people coming through its doors.' Although initially Linda did this work on a voluntary basis, the Church Urban Fund did eventually pay her a small salary.

And during this time of course she got to know Peter, the vicar. He first asked her to consider what God was calling her to do even before she began work as a community worker. 'I thought community work was my calling but I later discovered that Peter had seen it only as a stepping stone. He believed that my lack of church experience would have counted against me had I immediately gone forward for a selection conference within the Anglican Church. He never doubted my calling to ordained ministry but saw that I needed "Church" experience if I were to progress. The first time he mentioned it I was shocked – the only priests I had ever met had been men – even though I knew the Church of England ordained women.'

Nor, as it turns out, was Peter the only one to see her

path before she did. She remembers going to a big meeting which had been called to discuss ways of helping the community on the estate. 'And I lost my rag, I got really angry. I thought I've just got to say something here. And I did. I did a real rant. "How dare you sit here and tell these people what's good for them?" I told the meeting. "You come to Norris Green at nine o'clock and you go home at five. You don't live here. How do you know what it's like living on an estate like this? You don't. You've probably never lived anywhere like it. All you need to do is ask these people what they need and they'll do it themselves. They're not here to be helped and then off you go. They're the salt of the earth, these people. You *ask* them what they want, you don't *tell* them." I was really passionate. It had to be said.'

David Sheppard, the then Anglican Archbishop of Liverpool, was at the meeting and afterwards he asked her the same question that Peter had already put to her: Had she ever thought she might have a vocation to become a priest? 'I went "What do you mean? Me?"'

She continued being completely caught up in her community work, wondering how 'somebody like me, with my accent and from my background, could possibly become a priest'. One day there was a phone call from the local hospital. Her brother Michael had had an accident at work.

'I remember it clearly. It was a sunny Friday morning. Everything was normal. But it wasn't. Michael was on life support. Unconscious. The consultant said they were waiting for a miracle.

'I knew what to expect. I sat in the hospital chapel for hours. Peter was there some of the time. They came to talk to us about making a decision. About turning off the life support machine. I went back to the chapel. Dad came and sat with me. After a little while he said: "You're not going to get your miracle, Lin. Come on, we've got to get your

Mum through this." And we went back to Michael. Dad nodded to the nurse to turn off the machine. And he spoke to Michael. He said: "Go on son, you go now. You can go now."

'Mum was hysterical. Michael had been the favourite. A typical Liverpool lad. He was twenty-nine. She'd always spoiled him. We all spoiled him. I stayed in the chapel all that night crying and screaming at God, "Why, why, why?" I was so angry and so hurt. How could I believe in Him after this?

'I carried on going to church but I was just going through the motions. No one spoke about it. Nobody said anything. For a while Mum tried to spoil me like she had Michael, but I couldn't handle it. It was awful. They were both ... she was just walking about but ... it was awful. Awful.'

The first anniversary of Michael's death passed and nothing got any better. Shortly after that first anniversary Peter made her look at what was happening. '"You can't live your Mum and Dad's lives for them," he said. "Face it, face it square on: Michael's gone. And then start thinking again about ministry."'

At first she was angry that he'd spoken like that to her but as the days and weeks passed she came to understand that he was right. She couldn't live her Mum and Dad's lives for them. She had to go on living her own life.

Later she spoke to Peter about not being good enough for ordained ministry. 'But Peter didn't give up. I'd decided to go on retreat at Loyola Hall in Liverpool and as I went off to the retreat his parting comment was: "If you're waiting to be good enough then you'll have a long wait! None of us are good enough, but God still uses us all the same. It's through our weaknesses that God works – all he asks us to do is try. It's about time that you started pushing some doors to see which avenue God wants you to take."'

She had decided to go on the retreat to give herself time to see if she could find an answer to whether she should try for ordination. 'I had been reading Henri Nouwen and two of his books had influenced me particularly, *The Return of the Prodigal Son* and *Can You Drink the Cup?*, which was about vocation.' She falls silent for a few seconds, staring ahead of her, remembering. 'And I decided during that retreat that I could. I would try. I didn't think I'd get very far but I made the decision to apply.'

By this time she was receiving funding for her voluntary work, so had acknowledged church experience, but even so she still expected that the outcome of applying would be: '"Thanks very much, you're a good community worker but not ministry material." I mean, look where I was from. And I'd no education.'

The final part of the selection process was a residential weekend course where all the applicants were observed very closely.

'The first evening we had a role play exercise. We each got a problem to solve. Mine was that I had a church and outside all the local drug addicts congregated. Beside it there was an empty warehouse. What do you do? And I'm like "Wow. Great, that's where I live." I said, "Forget the church, we'll never get them in there. But what if the druggies are interested in music? A lot of them are. We'll form them into a band, use the empty warehouse as a rehearsal room, for performances, and as church as well. It'll be great."'

'And this guy with a proper accent – the opposite to me, you know – he said "We are told to bring people into the church, I hardly think this is a proper way to proceed." Well, that did it. I just completely lost it, told him what I thought about his stupid approach. What did he know about drug addicts, people living on the edge, no hopers whose mums and dads had probably never worked? I really let go. I ended by saying that I wasn't going to apologise later, either.'

Afterwards she thought, '"Well, Lin, you've really blown it now. You're supposed to be trying to impress these people so you can become a priest, and what do you do? The first night, the very first night, you have a rant, and a good 'un too. Well, there's no point in trying to impress them any-more, not after that. The church is paying for this weekend, I'll just enjoy myself. I can relax now and just be me." And I did, and I had a ball.'

She was selected unanimously. Which, she says, was a great lesson. 'It was like God was saying to me that I'd got a "Yes" because I had been myself. Like He was saying, be yourself, be who you are, that's all you have to be, be who you are. And I was stronger then.'

And she needed that strength when she went to theo-logical college. Not because of the studying, which she loved, 'even though it was really heavy' but because while the students' faith was being 'questioned from every angle' what made each of them individual was sometimes over-looked. There were times when she worried whether she had done the right thing.

One weekend she went back to Loyola Hall for a retreat. There she met John Hughes, a recently retired Franciscan. He was on a silent retreat but broke his silence to speak to her. 'He had a picture for me.' She smiles to herself, remem-bering. 'Not an actual picture. More an idea. The "picture" was a rucksack. And that made me smile because that was so me; a rucksack had been such a part of my life, travelling here and there. And the picture he showed me was of me not having to carry it all by myself.

'He didn't know I was an ordinand and when I told him

he just beamed and said: "I'd never have known. Is that a good thing or a bad thing?" And I said: "It's a good thing because I'm not going to become a pea in a pod, you know." And we both laughed. Right from the start we laughed together.' After that retreat John became her spiritual director.

'I really liked his idea of God. Now, how can I tell you his idea of God? Oh, I know. He told me a story from a book by Trevor Dennis called *The Three Faces of Christ*. This man turns up in Heaven and he's led a pretty bad life so he's not expecting to be there, you know. But he is expecting big pearly gates and all that but instead of gates and a palace he finds that God lives in a little terraced house and you have to go down an alleyway to get to the door. And when God opens the door she's wearing a pinny and has floury hands because she's baking bread. And she gives him a big hug and leaves two floury imprints of her hands on his back. And I could just imagine everybody in Heaven walking round with these two big floury imprints on their backs. And I just laughed; I thought it was wonderful.'

Her spiritual direction with John was never formal and there was always a lot of laughter. 'He just sort of kept me being me; he showed me that you can't be all "head", all academic, because you'd get so dry. Through him, with his help, I found a way to be at college and be myself at the same time.'

After college came the choice of her 'training' parish. The advice ordinands are given is not to look for someone they think they can get on with but to focus on finding a vicar who will give them good training.

The director of ordinands had profiles of various parishes for her to look at. 'Then he picked this particular one out, put it on the table in front of me and went off to make us a cup of tea while I read it. He gave a funny sort of smile as he left the room. I looked at this profile and thought "Wigan! Is Wigan still going?" And then I saw the name of the vicar was Kip and I thought, "What's he going to be like with a name like Kip?"'

But as she read the description of the parish she saw that this parish profile was different from the others; it had been put together in a very creative way. 'It was much less formal. He said how much he loved the people, and how much he loved the area. And I thought this is novel. I like this.'

So off to Ince, just outside Wigan, she went, to meet him. 'And as soon as I arrived Kip was just – he just radiated love. I could see why he'd written the profile the way he had. I knew almost instantly that I was going to come to Ince. His love for the people and the area was genuine, it just shone through him, I felt that straight away. And he's an artist, he loves to paint. And I felt here's someone who's creative and who can be my training vicar: I felt I had God's seal on this.'

She's well into her second year in Ince now and her initial feelings have been confirmed. She's had great training from Kip and complete support for her projects to take the church into the community. One of these is the celebration of Holy Communion at assembly in the local church school every few weeks. 'The children really love it, they love the singing, they really join in. And that is church for them. Some people got a bit upset, they thought I should be trying to get the children to come to church on Sundays. Well, no. Because I am going to them, in assembly. And that is church. Does it *have* to be in a church on a Sunday? In the morning? I think not. I am really keen to get away from the "bums on seats" mentality. It's the people we care about, not whether they come to a particular building.

'Kip has really supported me in all these sorts of projects, and these are things that can be delicate in a traditional parish like this. And he has also shown me – again – that being yourself is the most important thing. I mean – how can I put this – he's clumsy and he's forgetful but he's got such a heart, and a passion for the people he's serving. They love him and they work around him and help him. He's shown me that you're called to be yourself first, then a priest. God doesn't use the role, he uses the person, you, just as you are.'

And she, as a person, just happens to like candles. 'It's not a Catholic thing, but because they can set a mood.' So she introduced them in special services and has used them for morning and evening prayers, although, she adds, this is not a permanent fixture, yet.

'Well, you should have heard them. "Candles in church", they all gasped.' She grins, remembering the furore. 'But they were sort of joking too, you know, people were saying: "Candles in church! Mr Stoneley must be turning in his grave." But they were smiling when they said it, and they didn't mean it in a bad way.

'Mr Stoneley had been the vicar for a very very long time, some years before Kip became vicar,' she explains. 'A very powerful character he was, with very clear views. Very … traditional. But, seriously, Mr Stoneley did what he thought was right. You hear good stories about him as well as bad. It's just, you know, things change, don't they? It's a bit different now.'

Chapter 10

September 11 and my fear of flying

What a truly wondrous idea the siesta is. I sigh, deeply content. I am in a cool room at about three o'clock on a hot afternoon in Stoupa, a tiny resort in the Peloponnese. This morning I'd had a swim, read my latest Reginald Hill beneath an umbrella on the beach, we'd driven along the beautiful coast road to Kardamyli – mountains on the right, sparkling sea on the left, sunshine everywhere – for lunch and now here I am in this beautiful, peaceful room about to have my siesta. And twelve days of holiday to go. Bliss.

Ed bursts in, tension sparking off him like electricity.

'They say two planes have collided over New York.'

'Wha... I'm trying to have a nap. Are you sure? How could...?'

He grabs the remote, clicks on the television. Clouds of white smoke billow from two tall buildings; people wave white cloths from the windows. They're doing that to show us they're all right, I think to myself. The camera moves to the ground where tiny figures are running in panic, away from the white clouds which rush after them. Just like in *Independence Day*, the movie. What am I looking at? Is this real?

Later, like millions of others around the world, we learn from CNN news what has happened. Terrorists have hijacked planes and flown them into the World Trade Center. Thousands of people are dead. Dying. The brother of the man who owns the hotel we are staying in lives in America. He's here visiting at present; he can't get back now, all the flights have been cancelled. Bush is talking about war. Everybody is talking about who could have done such a thing. I remember the name of a very wealthy Arab terrorist from a couple of years ago. Laden or something.

My greatest fear, which I daren't put into words, is that the Americans will retaliate immediately in some way, and the world will be plunged into World War III. With nuclear weapons. The English papers, when they finally arrive, tell us of Blair's stance and I begin to wonder whether if, no, surely when, we get back home I will ever feel safe living in London again. And if I change my behaviour by one iota in response to that fear, the terrorists have won.

The rest of the holiday is punctuated by television news and reading the newspapers.

It's some sort of comfort to get a *Guardian* and a *Telegraph*; the tone is less terrifying than that of the American news on the television which makes me feel that war is very very near and that maybe we won't get home. I can't think about the people in the Trade Center; my mind pings off them, I can't think about it. When I read of the people in the aeroplanes being told to call home because they are going to die, I feel like I'm going to black out. How could anybody do … how could I sit in my seat in an aeroplane, borrow a mobile, and call and tell Ed that I love him, knowing I will never see him again, knowing that I am never going to leave this aeroplane, knowing that within hours I am going to be exploded to bits, burned to death…

During the Wednesday night before we are due to come home on the Sunday I lie in bed so afraid that I can't shut my eyes. I pray. I try to relax. I try to switch off the images. But I am sweating. My breathing is ragged. I can't even cry. If there's a war it could be something like the end of the world, mine and everybody else's. It could happen. It really could happen. If the Americans retaliate – with nuclear weapons, they've used them before – it could happen. Soon. So easily. God help me. I reach for Ed's hand. Sleepily, he asks if I'm OK.

'I'm so frightened I can't sleep.'

'It's OK, it'll be OK, you'll be fine.'

And after a while in fact I do sleep because the next thing I know it is morning. When we talk about it, Ed tells me he thought I was frightened of flying home because of what had happened. And that is part of it, but only a part of it.

On Friday night, having a shower before going out to eat, the fear coalesces around the thought of the moment of stepping into the plane and I start to cry. I cry for a minute or two then check myself. This is only making things worse, I need to keep the lid on this. And while it's all right having a good cry when you're young – your face recovers in seconds – when you're fifty-odd it takes ages to go down, then people can see you've been crying, then they get upset for you and then the whole evening's ruined. I let the shower run onto my face for a couple of minutes, and do some deep breathing.

Ed's turn to shower. The television is on as I dry myself. It's a concert in New York and I hear voices that are familiar to me, Clint Eastwood amongst them, so full of grief and passion that any covering of composure I'd managed is torn right through and I am once again in tears. All those people, husbands, wives, mums and dads, friends. This is unbearable, unbearable. The scene changes. What is this? Effigies of President Bush and of Tony Blair being thrust up into the air. Now the horrible effigy of Bush is burning and the turbanned men are screaming and shouting, beside themselves with rage, their eyes bulging with hatred. They hate Bush. The West. Us. Their rage is limitless, has limitless energy. The noise of their screams fills the room. I shut my eyes, feel dizzy, faint. I stumble for the remote control, and turn off the television. A couple of minutes later Ed comes out of the shower, wrapped in a towel, drying his hair.

'I think I had better not watch any more television please, and not read any more newspapers before we go home. It's ... it's ... I can't stand it. Everything I see, read – it's just too much for me.'

He nods, understanding, his glance full of concern.

'Might be best if we didn't talk about it anymore – it gets me just so, so ... it just makes it worse, I...'

I shake my head, I can't explain.

This tactic works and I have no more panic attacks or tears over the last couple of days of our holiday.

On Sunday at lunchtime we have a last beer in Kardamyli beneath the olive trees, by the sea, before setting off for the airport. In the little square by the church Ed stops the car. He wants to buy some of the purple and red shoelaces he saw the other day in the tiny shop on the corner. We have plenty of time. Off he goes. It is pleasant sitting there in the still Sunday lunchtime quiet.

Which is when it happens. One second I am fine, the next I am falling, falling, falling, faster and faster through bottomless blackness. The panic is all round me, all through me. So sudden, no defence, it's all around me, choking, suffocating, my limbs feel weightless, insubstantial. Lord help me. Even as I say the words, or rather hear them, somehow said in my mind, I feel sick with self-pity and wretchedness at the depths of my cowardice. I squeeze my eyes shut. I must control myself. Susie and David are in the back of the car. If I can't get control I'll be hysterical, unable to get on the plane. Stop. Stop the thoughts. What's this, what's this I'm seeing now? Me. It's me as a small child, a little girl, at the well; it's the image that first appeared at the retreat. I watch. There I am. There's the Christ figure. I am crying. He is almost crying himself as he reaches out and pulls me to him, stroking the top of my head, soothing me. He holds me, safe, until my tears cease.

The car door opens. I jump. I am back in the hot stillness of Sunday afternoon in Kardamyli. I examine my breathing. My limbs. I am fine. I am all right. I am calm and still.

We have pizza for lunch in Kalamata and drive to the airport. People are lying around everywhere, outside, inside, on the wide steps at the entrance to the airport. A bad sign: it means delays. But our flight, unlike the one which should have left three hours ago, is not late. In no time at all we are getting on the plane. And I am fine. I don't even marvel at this miracle, I just get on the plane. During the flight Susie and I play a favourite game of going over the Greek words she has learned on holiday, rehearsing a little conversation, checking the pronunciation and where to place the stress on the words. She has had a real problem with Monemvasia, the name of the thirteenth-century walled town where we spent a couple of nights during the first week of the holiday. The accent, the stress, needs to be on the final 'a' and for some reason the more she concentrates and the harder she tries the more scrambled the word becomes. She tries rushing it and saying it very fast. Then she takes a deep breath and tries it very very slowly. Hopeless. We both get the giggles. She pulls herself erect. Sits up very straight. Looks very serious and intent. Enunciates almost in slow motion. Turns to me for approval. It's worse than ever. We both crack up, tears streaming down our faces, incapable of speech, or of explaining to Ed and David just what is so incredibly funny.

It's not until we're home that I realise that you don't have a fit of the giggles, or real belly laughs, unless you are completely relaxed; it just doesn't happen when you're tense, when you're afraid.

Chapter 11

Listening for the heartbeat of God

> ... the Celtic tradition recognises our capacity for goodness; even when we fail we are seen as essentially good, as capable of not failing. Christ is portrayed as forgiving and 'full of grace'. God's goodness is at the heart of the human and humanity is graced with the profound desire to be holy, as God is holy. In repenting of sin we are not turning away in order to be someone else, but re-turning to our true selves, made in the loveliness and goodness of the image of God.[1]

I'd heard about Celtic spirituality before I read Philip Newell's *Listening for the Heartbeat of God*. I think it was a group of Quakers, talking after meeting for worship, who first used the phrase in my hearing. They seemed excited. I distrusted their enthusiasm. What the words suggested to me was something rather fey and suspiciously New-Age sounding. I dismissed it: not for me, this Celtic fringe. And I gave it no more thought.

When, years later, Linda Mary recommended this book to me she didn't mention the subtitle. It was only when I

[1] Philip Newell, *Listening for the Heartbeat of God: a Celtic Spirituality* (SPCK, 1997), p. 103.

bought it that I saw that the book was about Celtic spirituality. I quickly realised how misplaced my suspicion had been.

Philip Newell believes the Church, the world, all of us, are in need of the renewal and the refreshment this tradition has to offer. I agree with him. I know that I needed it; needed it without knowing that I had any need. Having finally found anger, and committed the metaphysical murder of the good old Uncle George image of God, and after a 35-year struggle with fear and guilt, I now needed what I had glimpsed during the retreat to be grounded. I needed that experience to be earthed in a wider context. And in this book I found it, not knowing I was looking for something or that there was anything to look for.

> The feature of Celtic spirituality that is probably most widely recognized, both within and outside the Church, is its creation emphasis. It was certainly this that first drew my attention. Like most children, I had grown up with a sense of awe at creation. Our earliest memories are generally of wonder in relation to the elements. Do we not all carry within us, for instance, something of the memory of first listening to the waters of a river or to rainfall, or lying in the grass, feeling and smelling it and seeing its brilliant green, or watching sunlight dappling through leaves? Connected to these moments will be recollections of experiencing at the deepest of levels a type of communion with God in nature, but there will usually have been very little in our religious traditions to encourage us to do much more than simply thank God for creation. The preconception behind this is that God is separate from creation. How many of us were taught actually to look for God within creation and to

recognize the world as the place of revelation and the whole of life as sacramental? Were we not for the most part led to think that spirituality is about looking away from life, so that the Church is distanced from the world and spirit is almost entirely divorced from the matter of our bodies, our lives and the world?[2]

Philip Newell was born and grew up in Ontario, Canada, the son of an Irish immigrant father, a minister in the evangelical Protestant tradition, and a Canadian mother whose own mother had come from Banffshire in Scotland. 'My granny's name was Mary Ferguson, and although she had lived in Canada for many many years, until the day she died at the age of ninety-six she still sounded as if she'd never left Cullen in Scotland.

'She lived with the family for almost ten years while I was at home. I have memories of coming home from school in my early teens with a girl from my class and my granny would meet us at the door and say something like: "Ain't love grand!" Which was embarrassing – naming what was happening.' He grins wryly as he recalls it.

'She'd a tremendous laugh in her. She loved laughter. I have a memory of sitting in church with her when I was a child. A person in the pew in front of us farted and of course, being a small boy, I thought it was hilarious – and my grandmother got the giggles as well.

'My experience of growing up with her around was that I was loved, and in a sense unconditionally loved. She treated me as if I could do no wrong. I mean, she knew I did things that were wrong, that I was often misbehaving in all sorts of ways. But she treated me much more as if she were dealing with the essence of me. She loved the heart of me.'

[2] ibid., p. 3.

His granny was not a great talker. Her influence on him was not through words but through her presence, who she was and how she was.

Later, in his teens, as he thought about his faith, it was memories of his grandmother that led to a moment of real illumination. A much respected colleague and friend of his father's, Dr Aidan Tozer, also played a part in this experience. Dr Tozer was a writer and considered a great preacher within the Evangelical Alliance tradition.

As an adolescent Philip began to feel an increasing discomfort with his faith. And at that stage 'his faith' meant Christianity as practised at the 'evangelical Protestant end of the spectrum'. He didn't know anything else. 'There was a heartfelt piety about it but its worldview was often fairly narrow. My experience growing up was that God was somehow specially present to people within this circle.'

Dr Tozer had been 'an honoured presence' among Philip's family since he was a small boy. 'He made a tremendous impression on me personally. I think he was a very shy man. At the end of the Sunday morning service, instead of going to the main door with my father to greet the congregation, he would go to his study. He always had sweeties and all the children would make for his study after service for the sweeties he had for us. At that time my great love was ice hockey, I played in goal, and my hero was Gump Worsley, the most famous goalie in ice hockey. Dr Tozer used to call me Gump Worsley and I just loved that, because there was nobody in the world I would rather have been than Gump Worsley.'

By the time he was beginning to explore the source of his religious discomfort in his mid-teens Dr Tozer was dead, but because of the happy memories Philip had of him he turned to his writings. 'What I discovered was that he had combined a sort of mysticism with evangelical piety. This was an unusual mixture of tremendous breadth. Much of the writing was about an awareness of the mystery of the presence of God. This resonated deeply within me. It helped me to articulate my dissatisfaction with the narrowness of the evangelical tradition and to see that often it portrayed the mystery of God in terms of judgement.'

He found that the starting-point of the evangelical tradition, as with so much of Western Christianity, was that what was deepest in humanity was sinfulness, original sin.

'So in this way of thinking the righteousness of God is such that a penalty payment has to be made. So essentially bad are we that there's nothing we can do to persuade the righteousness of God to be forgiving. Christ makes the payment that we cannot make.

'The moment of illumination came very much in terms of my grandmother. Because I realised that what this evangelical tradition was in effect saying was that my grandmother was more loving than God. What I experienced in my grandmother was this deep love and I couldn't find that same depth of love in the mystery of God. What was to the fore was the judgement – and of course the desire of God to forgive. But somehow, in this tradition, God couldn't be as forgiving towards me as my grandmother. God needed some sort of payment whereas I knew that my grandmother would freely forgive. That moment of illumination confirmed for me what I had sort of intuited earlier.'

It was around this same time of exploration of his faith that Philip began to read more widely. 'I sort of made the leap from ice hockey magazines to *Wuthering Heights* in one go. That was the novel we studied in school when I was fifteen going on sixteen. The book communicated a sense of mystery; it emotionally engaged me.'

His English Literature teacher at that time was David Creighton. 'He was the first teacher in my life who I felt engaged very directly and very deeply with his students. And he was the one who awakened my awareness of literature and poetry being a primary place of inspiration, which continues to this day.

'It was in his class that there came a "clicking" realisation that literature, at least in part, was about writing about the human soul: it was about giving expression to what is deepest in the human mystery; these texts related to the inner universe.'

David Creighton was also great at encouraging creative writing. So pleased was he with a piece that Philip wrote that he had him read it out to the class, which came as a great surprise to Philip. He'd chosen to write about a religious moment in the evangelical tradition. He described a service at which Dr Tozer had preached. 'But I wasn't trying to capture what had been said but to capture the atmosphere in its religious context. I can't remember much about what I wrote now except that it was peppered with humour. There was a bit of taking off of some of the piety, but it wasn't entirely without seriousness.'

He learned three valuable lessons from this: he enjoyed writing; he began to have more confidence in the imagination as a way of knowing; and he realised he took a delight in humour and the absurd.

He was also very good at sciences, however, and well before he was eighteen it had been decided he would become a doctor. Although there were readers in his family, the hard-working, working-class families from which his mother and father came couldn't see how literature would bring him a living so there was 'nothing that particularly encouraged me to follow my heart on the literature front'. He applied, quite happily, to read medicine at the University of Toronto and was accepted.

Then during the spring of his last year at school

something happened. He and three of his friends went up to a cabin in the Muskoka Lakes district where he'd spent every summer at a church camp run by his father. This year they decided to go up few days early.

None of them were inclined to religious reflection. But somehow the conversation after the evening meal turned to a sense of dissatisfaction with their evangelical tradition; there was a sense that some very deep and heartfelt searching was going on. After they'd been talking for some time one of them suggested they pray.

'This was something that had never happened before, this suggestion that we pray. Of course all of us had been present at many prayer events but never had anybody initiated prayer like this, outside of a structured context. As we began to pray – I don't think I had uttered anything in prayer, although a couple of the lads had – I became aware of a great presence of light. And I was so over-whelmed by the sense of light and also of love that I began to laugh. But it wasn't laughing *at* anything, it was pure delight, an experience of pure delight. I began to laugh, feeling so free that I simply didn't think it might be blasphemous or wrong to laugh in the context of prayer. I was so ... I just wouldn't have been able to stop myself. And then the others had the same experience. So the four of us just laughed and laughed for probably over ten minutes, which is a long time. We came out of prayer mode through the laughter because prayer mode in our tradition was heads bowed and eyes closed and praying in words. What we were having was a religious experience of laughter. There were tears afterwards from two of the fellows. We all had the feeling of having received a tremendous gift, we knew something deeply authentic had happened but we had no way of making sense of it.'

Afterwards, when he talked to his father about this

experience, he found that although his father had never had such an experience himself, 'he was immediately open to affirming it.

'One of the reasons my father has always been a very important person for me is that he's a man of the heart; an awareness and sensitivity at the heart level has always been there with my father.' Over the weeks that followed the weekend at the Muskoka Lakes, and arising directly from the 'religious laughter', he began to feel disturbed about his choice of medicine as a career and seriously to doubt whether that was the right path for him. His thoughts turned to theology but that couldn't be studied as a first degree. But what of his love of English literature? Why not do that as a first degree? When he began to tell his father of his decision not to do medicine he broke down and wept because he thought his father, and indeed all the family, would be so disappointed in him. Instead, he found the opposite, a very ready acceptance of the change.

'The decision not to go for medicine was a tremendous relief. I realised it had been a head-related thing. Once I'd set it aside I was able to see that what I really loved was literature. This was the beginning of a wonderful period of study for me.'

His head of department at McMasters University, Hamilton was Douglas Duncan. Duncan had grown up in Scotland, the son of the principal of a theological college, though he himself had rejected any formal ties with religion. In his second year Philip was in Douglas Duncan's tutorial group. 'He was a great teacher and he strongly affirmed the sort of work I was doing in literature, which was to use it as a tool for inner exploration.'

At the same time Philip's awareness of justice issues was increasing and he would organise 24-hour student fasts, the money raised by sponsorship going to feed the hungry.

'Douglas was aware of this combination in me, of the justice issues and the way I was working in literature, and this resonated deeply with him. He encouraged me and we became and remain good friends.'

> There are some who call themselves Christian, and who attend worship regularly, yet perform no Christian actions in their daily lives. There are others who do not call themselves Christian, and who never attend worship, yet perform many Christian actions in their daily lives. Which of these two groups are the better disciples of Christ? Some would say that believing in Christ and worshipping him is what matters for salvation. But this is not what Jesus himself said. His teaching was almost entirely concerned with action, and with the motives which inspire action. He affirmed the goodness of behaviour in whoever he found, whether the person was Jew or Roman, male or female. And he condemned those who kept all the religious requirements, yet were greedy and cruel. Jesus does not invite people to become his disciples for his own benefit, but to teach and guide them in the ways of goodness. And if a person can walk along that way without ever knowing the earthly Jesus, then we may say that he is following the spirit of Christ in his heart.[3]

When, in 1975, having completed his English Literature degree, he went to Edinburgh to study theology he came under the influence of another important teacher, Alec Cheyne. 'He used to say to us that if we couldn't be brilliant we could at least be lucid. He taught me a lot about the need

---

[3] ibid., quoting Pelagius, p. 18.

for clarity in writing. He was also perceptive enough to realise that an essay I wrote about the emergence in nineteenth-century Scotland of a spirituality that was seeking breadth and connection had really captured my heart and mind. I identified with those nineteenth-century spirituality reformers, which is what they were, and their struggle to find something new, to escape from the very closed form of Calvinism that was so dominant at that time. In doing that they were reflecting my own journey and Alec saw that.'

With encouragement from Alec Cheyne he began to focus on this 'gang of Scottish reformers' and one name began to appear again and again: Alexander Scott. He had written very little and no one knew much about him. At Alec Cheyne's suggestion Philip decided to stay on and do a PhD on the nineteenth-century Scottish reformers, and to see if there was enough about Alexander Scott to form the basis of a thesis.

He discovered a huge collection of letters to people such as Thomas Carlyle, Charles Ruskin, Frederick Chopin and Charles Dickens. He also discovered that there had been a crisis in Alexander Scott's life when he was still a young man which led to him being thrown out of the Church for heresy. 'In order to be ordained he had to sign the Westminster Confession of Faith, which was the primary doctrinal expression of belief in the Church of Scotland. One of the core beliefs expressed in it is that humanity has been made the opposite to all good. Humanity in this Calvinistic tradition is seen as being essentially evil. It's a document that rips apart the mystery of creation. Alexander Scott refused to sign it. But instead of then stepping down from seeking ordination he appealed to the highest ecclesiastical court in Scotland, the General Assembly. He argued for his beliefs before this court, in

1831. The three hundred or so ministers who formed the membership of the court rejected his teachings unanimously.

'After the heresy trial he moved to London. A series of public lectures he gave on subjects such as the spirituality of science, the spirituality of music and the spirituality of literature showed him to be a mystic who was drawing together the various threads of life as he looked for a new way of religion.

'In an exact contradiction of Calvinism Scott believed that what is deepest within us is the image of God. He also believed that what he was re-discovering in the old Celtic Christian tradition, which was older than Mediterranean Christianity, was extremely valuable and needed to be brought into the life of the Church. What he saw in the old Celtic tradition was this tremendous sense of creation as showing, as revealing, the mystery of God. Of course he didn't call what he was doing Celtic spirituality but he was drawing from that well which we now refer to more explicitly as the Celtic stream.'

Philip recognised that Scott's rejection of Calvinism and his turning towards the old Celtic tradition in Christianity mirrored the direction in which he himself, over a century later, was moving. 'I identified with him personally. I came to know him and to love him. He was an inspirational figure for me.'

At the beginning of his research into the life and theology of Scott Philip married a fellow student, Alison, and together with some others they set up a small residential community in Plimpton, a very poor and run down council estate tucked away in a northern corner of Edinburgh. They negotiated with the council for each of the six couples to have a flat in the same building with a common landing so they would be a community.

All of them made a commitment to live there for three

years and to try and find replacements when they left. They had no clear idea of what they were going to do, just a desire, partially inspired by Alison's experience of the Iona Community's concern with practical justice, to be where people were in need, to be amongst the poorest of the poor. Some members of the community became active in local politics, others concentrated on issues to do with, for instance, housing or rents. The only pattern the group set themselves was to pray together each day at six o'clock, the prayer to take the form decided upon by whoever was hosting the prayers that evening. The meetings were open to anyone who wanted to come and were followed by tea, coffee and biscuits.

At first the people on the estate were completely baffled by the group having chosen to come to Plimpton, since they were all desperately trying to get away from the place. But as the young couples began to start their families – Philip and Alison's first child, their daughter Rowan, was born there – the new babies and toddlers quickly became points of contact. Children began to drop in, some of them started to come to the prayer time; perhaps for the prayer but, being children, perhaps also for the tea and biscuits which followed.

'There was one young lad who used to come along quite regularly. Young James. He was about eight or nine. One of the strangest faces I'd ever seen; his eyes looked in different directions, so he was very strange to look at. Most of the time he was filthy, smelly and unwashed. He used to like to come to prayers. And this particular day he arrived a little late. The focus for the prayer that day was an icon of the mother and child which we'd placed on the mantelpiece. And when young James arrived there was only one place left where he could sit, a small stool beside the mantelpiece. So he sat ... and he was sitting facing the group. And everybody was looking at the icon. But, in part because he had a sight difficulty, he thought we were looking at him. And he began to smile, with this extraordinary strange little face. And of course, at that moment, he became the icon. And you had this wonderful experience of seeing all the strain leave his face.'

It was while they were living in Plimpton that Philip met George MacLeod, the founder of the Iona Community, who was already a friend of Alison's. George MacLeod founded the community in 1938, as an ecumenical community which seeks new ways of living the Gospel in today's world. It's committed to 'rebuilding the common life' through working for social and political change, to the renewal of the Church with an ecumenical emphasis, and to exploring new more inclusive approaches to worship, all based on a spirituality centred on the self *and* others.

Off Iona the community has a pattern of cells of around ten people who meet regularly; Philip and Alison were in George MacLeod's family group because he lived not far from Plimpton.

'As I began to get to know George MacLeod I came to see that he was a living expression of the mysticism of Alexander Scott and of the perspectives provided by the Celtic tradition. The prayers he uttered, for example about the eternal seeping through the physical, resonated deeply with me. And of course, linked with the creation spirituality was the passion for justice.'

> MacLeod ... was clearly not tempted away from action by study. Instead, he was always drawn to be part of the immediate flow of life, and intuitively to grasp in his normal daily routine the Life that is within all life and at the heart of every moment. He wrote:

> It is the primacy of God as Now that we must recover
> in Christian mysticism ... When in the morning we
> get to our desk, that list of meetings, the whole design
> of the day's life as it builds up from this or that tele-
> phone call, the person we like whom we are to meet
> at four, the person more difficult to like who will
> come at five ... Get through the day we are apt to say,
> and then perhaps at nine o'clock tonight, or nearer
> perhaps to eleven, we can have our time with God.[4]

At the end of their time in Plimpton an invitation came for
Philip to become chaplain at his old university, McMaster,
in Canada. During their six years there Philip worked to
develop an ecumenical community at the heart of the chaplaincy and, when the US closed its borders to political
refugees from Central America, turned the chaplaincy into
a welcoming point for the refugees. A young woman from
Guatemala, Rosa, became the nanny to their second child,
Brendan, and soon afterwards, to their third child, Kirsten.

'Welcoming people, hearing their stories, and helping to
settle them around Hamilton, you really experienced the
goodness of making the connection between the inner life
and the outer life. Making that connection was the real
thrust of the chaplaincy.'

So, when he and Alison, who was now also ordained,
were asked if they would like to take on the job of being the
wardens at Iona Abbey, they didn't hesitate: 'It felt
absolutely right.'

They arrived on the island in May 1988 with Rowan,
aged eight, Brendan, aged six, and Kirsten a babe in arms.
'There was something about the light there – like Greek
light – and a crispness to colours; it was – George MacLeod

---

[4] ibid., p.80.

used to describe it as a very thin place, you know ... there's something about living on an island, the water, being on the edge of an immensity.'

He breaks off and smiles at the near impossibility of conveying the atmosphere and feeling of the place. 'And it was a good place for the children; they loved it. But I did wonder afterwards – they had so much freedom, we were so caught up in the abbey – I did wonder if the absence of more family time together had been good for them.'

His feelings about his own experience of nearly four years on Iona are similarly mixed. He describes that time as both intensely inspiring and totally exhausting. On the one hand there was the feeling of being highly inspired to be on the island where Columba had founded a monastery in 563, an island that was such a central part of the ancient Celtic tradition, the island of George MacLeod, a place to which people came from all over the world, sometimes, like the ANC students from South Africa before its liberation, bringing with them a lot of pain.

But on the other hand, as the warden, at the top of the administrative structure, with a big staff to manage and a hundred new people a week arriving, the pace of life was terrific; where was the time for solitude? 'I hated aspects of the wardenship, I didn't feel that I was playing to my strengths. And the life of the Iona community means lots of people being together a lot. I had some difficult times.'

He totally accepted the need to make the connection between spirituality and justice but wanted to bring more emphasis onto the question of 'how we were developing our contemplative side, our disciplines of solitude'. But, of course, there wasn't much time for that, which was 'a constant frustration' for him.

The answer to his dilemma, though that is not how it seemed at the time, came in the form of Harry Underhill, who spent a lot of time on Iona. 'I wouldn't want to put this in terms of Harry wanting to teach the Iona community anything, because he's too humble a guy for that. But – anyway, what happened was he felt it would be good for me to have some experience of the East so he provided two tickets and he and I went to India for three weeks, to the ashram of Bede Griffiths, a Benedictine monk who had spent most of his life in India.'

Philip had read one of Bede Griffith's books, *The Marriage of East and West,* before Harry suggested the trip so he knew already that Bede's foremost vision was of Western Christianity's need to learn from the East 'in terms of mysticism and meditation. Bede felt the Gospel of Christ needed to be stripped of its Western robes and clothed in Eastern dress.'

During their first night in India, in Madras, he had a dream. In the dream he was having a drink with Mikhail Gorbachev. As Philip drained his glass he saw that there was a chemical deposit or something like that in the bottom of the glass: Gorbachev had drugged him or perhaps even poisoned him.

He interpreted this as revealing a powerful unconscious resistance to the East, to the unknown. Gorbachev was to the East of the Western world, a figure both powerful and different. They are having a drink together so they are behaving like friends. But then comes Philip's discovery that he might have been deceived.

'The dream helped me to understand there was a question mark over the East for me. Up to that stage my form of spirituality had been very Western, related to liturgy and prayer, word-centred. I had no knowledge of meditation or of the discipline of silence. So while at one level I was eager to experience India, at another level there was some deep anxiety.'

On the morning of the first day at the ashram, which seemed to him to be like a walled garden, full of flowers and rich with scents, he woke before sunrise and made his way to the central building for the first designated meditation session of the day. The second was at sunset.

He took his place in the dark room; there were only a few candles for light, and sat on a mat on the floor amongst many other people. 'But I didn't have the tools to meditate, I didn't know how.' He spent the first day trying to make sense of the rhythm of the place. And he learned that Bede had recently suffered a severe stroke; there was fear that he might die. The stroke had happened during meditation. However, Bede would see them in a day or two, for a few minutes.

That evening he walked by the river which flowed beside the ashram with an old monk. He asked the monk to tell him about meditation. The monk explained that one of the most practised ways of meditation in their community was to take a phrase, usually from Scripture, something that stayed in your mind when you read a passage of Scripture, and simply repeat it. Over and over. Like a mantra. 'The monk said that the mind took us all over the place, while meditation seeks to still us in the present.'

The next morning, sitting by the river this time rather than indoors, Philip began to do this. 'And I took to it immediately. A phrase strikes your mind because the unconscious has recognised it. There was the rhythm of the phrase and a deepening. Very simple. So ... it felt like coming home to something.'

He met Bede the following day. 'His countenance was bright and he was full of questions about Iona. He didn't have a terrific amount to say but his presence made a tremendous impression on me.'

He stares out of the window for a moment into the pale

spring sunlight of the Edinburgh morning, so different from the heat and the exoticness of the ashram at Shantivanam.

'Part of the pattern of the day was to have a siesta for a couple of hours after lunch. During the siesta on the third day I had a brief but highly significant dream. A beautiful woman came to me and said "My mother tells me that I have always loved you." And I woke up with this over-whelming sense of being loved, of love. At first, trying to understand the dream I thought that maybe the woman was the Church or the religious community. But then on further reflection I thought of her in terms of the anima, the femi-nine principle. But – "my mother tells me" – that was pointing to something beyond herself. It was pointing towards the feminine. And when I realised this I wept and wept. And the weeping was very – it was very sort of puri-fying of the spirit. It wasn't the idea of the feminine that brought me to tears so much as the deep love.

'This experience showed me that – it was as if something very deep was stirring and the discovery of the meditation practice was part of it, almost preparation for it. It was almost as if I'd been too busy before, both inside and out-side; as if I had to go on this long journey to the East, be in this enclosed garden, learn about meditation and only then, during the siesta, was I free to let go and experience this.'

It was only much later that he learned of an extra-ordinary coincidence: something similar had happened to Bede, during his 'stroke' a few days earlier. 'When Bede began to speak about what had happened he said that he had seen the divine in feminine terms. And although Bede had been in the East for many years his Christianity was nevertheless still so deeply Western that when he experi-enced the mystery in feminine terms it shook him to his foundations.'

Once back on Iona Philip began editing and writing *The Iona Community Worship Book*. But unlike his earlier, academic writing, which had relied heavily on research, this time he was writing from the heart. 'Things began to come together now; I realised how much I wanted to write.'

A year later, in 1992, they left Iona and returned to Alison's family flat in Edinburgh, where he was given the opportunity to spend time writing by Gilleasbuig Macmillan, the minister of St Giles Cathedral. He had known Gilleasbuig since he was a student and had always felt very attracted by what he had heard 'uttered' at the cathedral, so had no hesitation in accepting when Gilleasbuig invited him to be part of the team, and to concentrate on shaping worship and liturgy. It was only after he'd been back in Edinburgh for some while that he realised how utterly depleted, how exhausted, he had been when he left Iona.

One of the things he began was a daily, early morning Communion service at the cathedral. 'Often it would begin in darkness and there would be only two or three people. To have just a few people – instead of hundreds. That was wonderful. My word, that was wonderful.'

As his energies returned he once again began to write and to dig back more consciously into the Celtic tradition. 'I had this realisation that here was treasure that I must unpack. On Iona I had been too busy running things, but now, back in Edinburgh, this was the place.'

Listening for the Heartbeat of God drew on his experience as an academic researcher but rather than being an academic book, which he knew he didn't want to write, was written, like the *The Iona Community Worship Book*, from his heart.

In 1995 the family moved south when Philip was appointed Warden of Spirituality, a newly created post, in Portsmouth. This was basically a teaching, preaching, and writing post. Apart from running courses at the centre and giving talks and lectures, the focus of his time in Portsmouth was twofold: the creation of the walled garden around the house as a place of meditation and peace in the centre of a busy city, and the writing of more books. 'This time in England was a time of great creativity; there was a tremendous receptivity throughout the diocese to what I was trying to do.'

They returned to Edinburgh in 2000 when Alison was appointed the head of the spirituality programme at the Scottish churches' open college. By now Philip was very much aware how important writing was to him. Recognising this and the value of what he was trying to do, Gilleasbuig created the position of scholar in spirituality at the cathedral for him, so that he could concentrate on writing, free of the demands of pastoral duties.

In February 2002 he went to Canada and Alaska to follow up a burgeoning interest in the interconnection between Celtic spirituality and Native or First Nation spirituality. An event had been organised by an ecumenical collection of churches and the organiser, knowing of Philip's interest in this area, invited him to meet some members of the Sturgeon Lake tribe of the Cree people and to take part in a sweat lodge experience.

The sweat lodge is made of branches of trees which are covered with animal skins. There is a radius of about five feet from the centre, and the height inside is about five feet also. A flap covers the entrance. In the centre of the sweat lodge there is a hole in the ground which is filled with rocks which have been heating for two days.

'I was met by seven Cree elders, tremendous characters, weathered, almost leathered, faces. They were old except for one who was about forty-five. They struck me as having a great humility about them and they had a generous hospitality towards me. This was very much part of the importance of the experience for me because their culture has been so abused, so fragmented at the hands of white European aggression – and European Christianity was a part of that aggression. Here were these people, whose society today has terrible problems of poverty, alcoholism, terrible deprivation, who were so wronged by our ancestors and yet they were so hospitable, so receiving of me.

'The event began with one of the elders saying a few words in English to me. He said his name was Paul Dreaver and his great-great-grandfather was Harry Dreaver from the Orkney Islands, so he too was Scottish but he chose to express his spirituality through his Cree side. We smoked the peace pipe then and afterwards were joined by two Cree women elders.'

The host elder said they weren't going to tell him anything about the sweat lodge ceremony, they simply wanted him to experience it. 'Partly that was because of their humility: they didn't want to appear to be my teachers, but part of it was also not wanting, through the use of words, to shape my expectations. All I knew was that there would be four sessions, or rounds, as they described them, of about twenty minutes each.

'Once inside the sweat lodge we all sat down on the ground. It was pretty crowded and as it turned out I was grateful for that because for quite a lot of the time my body was propped up by the people on either side of me. You could just see the glow from the hot rocks but otherwise we were in total darkness.

'As the highest point of the lodge was only five feet it didn't take long to get very hot. Sweat lodge is a bit of a misnomer, burn lodge would be better because the experience is of intense heat. You feel like you're burning from the head down. It starts at the top. And the effect is to make you lean forward to get as close as possible to the ground as you can, because it might be a bit cooler there. So … there's this humbling movement of bowing down to the earth. There were drumbeat and rattle sounds and chanting. And the heat got more and more intense. And quite a lot of shouting of 'oh, oh, oh'. And part of that – that blowing out, that strong exhaling, is because you can't take it any more without making that noise. And the chanting becomes more and more and more intense until, just when you feel you can't take it anymore, you'll have to get out, the flap comes up.

'It was made clear to me that I could go outside after each round, which I did. But the elders stayed in the sweat lodge, chanting, singing, the drums beating. As I stood there after that first twenty minutes I wondered whether I was going to be able to endure it.

'The second round had a slightly different feel to it. When I went outside after the second round I told the host elder that I thought I was going to black out; I was going to be sick and black out. He gave me a cup of ice cold water. And at that point he chose to speak, out of my need and weakness. He said, "Your body is trying to tell you that it is in control, but our body is not our deepest centre. When you go back you might find your mind is trying to tell you that it is in control, but our mind is not our deepest centre. What we are seeking in the sweat lodge is to return and to connect with what is at the centre of our being, of everything. That is the place of control." And these words were immensely important to me. And I was so struck by the fact that he had not chosen to speak until I needed him to speak. And also at this time a young man spoke to me. He explained that the first round had been towards the West, its colour was black. Going towards the West you went into the darkness. The second round, that had just finished, had been in the direction of the North. Its colour was white, it was a place of stillness. So having gone into the darkness, gone down into the darkness of the West, which was like death, you waited in that place, in stillness. He said that when I went back in I would be fine because the third round, whose colour was gold, was in the direction of the East, and was about birth and healing. The fourth round, whose colour was blue, was in the direction of the South and was about new beginnings, new life.

'And he was right, I was fine. Oh the heat was still intense, I was still trying to hug the ground to get as close to it as possible but – truly the place I was at was not physical ... was not mental. It was something – the experience was within, something fundamental.'

After the fourth round when it was all over and all he wanted to do was lie down he asked what had been being uttered in the chanting. 'The silence then was total. And I thought maybe I'd asked something they didn't reveal. But then, finally, after at least a minute of silence, the oldest elder, who was still inside the lodge, spoke. He said: "We were praying for you. And for your people."'

Later Philip remembered some words of a Mohawk elder who had spoken to him a few days earlier. 'He said he wondered where we would have been today if the Christian mission that had come from Europe had been part of the Celtic tradition of Christianity, which would have respected his people's spirituality. He said "they could have flowed together".'

Chapter 12

Greece again, but not on holiday

'You're always complaining about the weather and the tax-man and the government in England, why don't you come to Greece for the summer and work in the bar for me?'

Antony made this offer to my husband Ed in 2001. It was during a typically Greek-extended New Year's Day lunch at our flat in Richmond. The whole family were there: Antony, Valerie, his wife, who is English, and their three children, Phillip, eight, Louise, six and Annie, our goddaughter, aged two.

The kids were watching the video of *A Bug's Life*, one of their Christmas presents from us – a not entirely dis-interested choice: we knew that come New Year's Day, the bugs would give us half a chance for a bit of peace.

At the time Antony made his suggestion I was talking to Valerie about the vastly superior shopping pleasure to be had in England as compared with Zakynthos. She was bemoaning the facts that there were no department stores, and that as soon as you walked into a, usually small, shop the proprietor would be onto you immediately, demanding to know what you wanted. No escape was possible and therefore there was no time for proper shopping, let alone bargain-hunting. Valerie is Olympic standard at bargain-hunting.

However, as often happens when something is mooted in an adjacent conversation which might affect you, you tune into it, albeit unconsciously. Which is just what I did when I heard Antony's invitation to Ed to come and work at the Driftwood.

I didn't have to listen any longer to know what Ed's answer would be. The logo of the Driftwood is the cartoon character, the Mexican mouse, Speedy Gonzales: Ed has Speedy, plus hat, plus the name of the bar, tattooed, in red, yellow and black, on his left buttock. Nothing was going to stop us packing up and going to Greece for the summer. And I knew that any negativity and tedious nitpicking on my part about paying the mortgage and pension contributions; my job; what *I* would do over there; what I would do over there without the local library, would be dismissed with a truly Greek lift of the shoulders by Ed. And they were. Eventually.

I staved it off for two years. But why, I asked myself often, was I so reluctant? I was the Graecophile who'd introduced Ed to Greece on our overland trip in 1972. So why the hanging back? The upheaval of renting the flat, decorating, the expense etc., was part of it: loving my life in Richmond was part of it. And a big part of it was that Laganas in 2001 was not the Laganas we had discovered in 1985. Now Zakynthos was the third most popular Greek island after Rhodes and Corfu. Laganas' high street was all bars (one called Potter's Bar, the name printed across a tube station logo), neon-emblazoned discos and fast-food places. And of course, yards of souvenir shops. You could eat at McDonalds but you'd have to look very hard for good Greek cooking. Very hard. Where there had been no lager louts, now there were plenty. You could stand in the main street and not know where in the world you were. It was hot and the sea was at the bottom of the road but you had little way of knowing you were in Greece. All of those things weighed on me but finally I concluded that at bottom I was afraid of such a big change. I was, in fact, afraid of change.

I read Margaret Guenther's book, *Toward Holy Ground,* around this time and its sympathetic and sensible approach to middle age (and late middle age) fears helped. Also, one Sunday, on the noticeboard at the meeting house, I saw there was a postcard which showed part of the Quaker tapestry, which depicts Quaker history. It spoke of the Quaker admonition to 'live adventurously'. Oh well, I thought, maybe this move to Greece is timely, part of getting used to change. But I wasn't convinced.

I asked the people for whom I do a lot of work as a copy editor if they had any objection to me working from Greece, which information technology now made possible. They didn't. What a relief! At least I would still be earning while we were away. We began to make plans. My reluctance, which amounted, at times, to something very like dread, didn't go away.

We managed – at the last minute – to rent the flat, a financial necessity, and arrived on the island with laptop and printer in tow just in time to attend the Easter service at midnight in the courtyard of the family's local village church. Which was great, but later …

On Ed's second day working in the bar at the Driftwood the cook, Anne, fell off her moped, hurt her knee badly and couldn't walk. So Antony had to go into the kitchen to cover for her which meant Ed had to work seven days a week in the bar. For about seven weeks. Then the heatwave started. It lasted for three months. Ed was working in 50°C and going through three t-shirts a day. I was sweltering in a rented house with the windows and doors closed against the flies and two fans failing to keep me cool. Meanwhile, there were big technological changes going on at work as we changed word processing systems, IT systems, and typesetters, while I was doing two journals simultaneously. Then, on deadline for the two journals, still struggling to master the technology, I got the Blaster virus. Twice. You don't thumb through the Yellow Pages on a Greek island to get computer help. Even if there were Yellow Pages. Even if you could read them in Greek.

As a result of all this I began to have real problems sleeping and lost quite a lot of weight. My dilemma was professional and financial: my professional conscience said 'you will meet all deadlines' but without a functioning PC and mastery of the technology, how could I? If I lost my job because of this, with Ed earning very little at present, what would happen? I had been fearful of working in Greece; my fears had been justified.

Once home things didn't get any better. A friend who is a GP rang one day and during our conversation asked if I thought I was depressed. I said of course I was. He asked about sleeping and moods. I said that sleeping had been a problem for months and that I was tearful every day. He suggested I see my GP and ask for anti-depressants; a talking therapy might take too long, I needed help quickly. So, as a result of the stress while in Greece I was now on anti-depressants. I didn't know I was on Prozac until a detective in a TV series said a suspect had 'fluroxetine – that's Prozac to you and me – beside his bed'. It was a shock. Somehow being on Prozac made me think of myself as a different sort of person from one who was merely on anti-depressants. Which told me that I was still thinking about people in categories: is there 'a kind of person who is on Prozac'?

Shortly after going to see my GP I made the decision, with her support, to see if I could get rid of some of my copy editing workload. This turned out to be acceptable to my employers and so from March 2004 I had a reduced amount of work to do. Which was just as well because as I write I am within a week of returning to Greece for five months. It feels very like how I imagine a novice rider feels when advised to get straight back on the horse that has just thrown her over its head. However, I have just cut my Prozac intake by half and I am feeling fine. But I can't help thinking of one of the stories Steve McQueen's character tells in *The Magnificent Seven*, when asked how preparations to deal with the bandit gang are going: 'So far, so good, as the man said as he fell past the seventh-storey window...'

Resources

Barclay, William. *A Plain Man Looks at the Beatitudes*. London: Fount, 1985.

Cameron, Julia. *The Vein of Gold: A Journey to Your Creative Heart*. London: Pan, 1997.

Fox, M. *Original Blessing*. New York: Penguin Putnam, 2000.

Guenther, M. *Toward Holy Ground: The Art of Spiritual Direction*. London: Darton, Longman and Todd, 1996.

Hughes, G. W. *God of Surprises*. London: Darton, Longman and Todd, 1985.

—*In Search of a Way*. London: Darton, Longman and Todd, 1986.

—*Walk to Jerusalem*. London: Darton, Longman and Todd, 1991.

—*Oh God, Why?* Oxford: The Bible Reading Fellowship, 1993.

—*God, Where Are You?* London: Darton, Longman and Todd, 1997.

—*God of Compassion*. London: CAFOD and Hodder and Stoughton, 1998.

—*God in All Things*. London: Hodder and Stoughton, 2003.

Küng, H. *On Being a Christian*. London: William Collins and Sons Ltd, 1978.

—*Does God Exist?* London: William Collins and Sons Ltd, 1980.

Kazantzakis, N. *Report to Greco*. London: Faber and Faber, 1973.

Newell, P., *Listening for the Heartbeat of God: a Celtic Spirituality*. London: SPCK, 1997.

Nouwen, H., *The Return of the Prodigal Son*. London: Darton, Longman and Todd, 1992.

—*Can You Drink the Cup?* Notre Dame, IN: Ave Maria Press, 1996.

Quaker Faith and Practice. London: The Yearly Meeting of the Religious Society of Friends (Quakers) in Britain, 1995.

Silf, M. *Landmarks: an Ignatian Journey*. London: Darton, Longman and Todd, 1998.